APPEAL

HOW TO CAST DARK SPELLS OF REVENGE, CURSING & DAMNATION

GREGORY LEE WHITE

White Willow Press
Nashville, TN

Hex Appeal
How to Cast Dark Spells of Revenge, Cursing, and Damnation
by
Gregory Lee White

Copyright © 2022 Gregory Lee White
gregoryleewhite.com

No part of this publication may be reproduced, distributed, or transmitted in any form or by any means, including photocopying, recording, or other electronic or mechanical methods, without the prior written permission of the publisher. All rights reserved.

Text:
Gregory Lee White

Cover Art:
Margaret Brundage & Gregory Lee White
Cover of the pulp magazine *Weird Tales* (March 1937, vol. 29, no. 3)

Proofreading:
Gregory Lee White, Roy Hamilton, Virginia Tabor, Carolina Dean

Interior Illustrations:
various artists and illustrators from 1880 to the 1930s

First Edition 2022

Published by
White Willow Press
211 Donelson Pike, Suite 111
Nashville, Tn 37214

Printed in the United States

ISBN: 978-1-7379306-3-1

TABLE OF CONTENTS

What is a Hex?	1
Person, Place, or Object?	3
The Ancestral Curse	5
Baneful or Coercive Oils	7
Curses Around the World	9
Famous Curses	15
Curses as a Plot Device	25
Should You Hex Someone?	33
Is it Justified?	36
Laying Tricks	43
Candle Magic	58
Baneful Herbs and Notions	65
Hexes and Cursing Spells	69
Banishing Spells	72
Spells of Revenge and Sorrow	77
Sexuality Curses	85
Financial Ruin	87
Liars and Gossips	89
Love Life Hexes	90
Commanding and Controlling Spells	92
Confusion Spells	95
Spells of Sickness	98
Bad Luck Spells	100
Unhexing	103
Warding Off Evil	111
Protective Amulets	118
Stones for Protection	119
Spells to Uncross	127
Protection Spells	130
Conclusion	138
Bibliography	139

OTHER BOOKS BY GREGORY LEE WHITE

Clucked – The Tale of Pickin Chicken

Making Soap from Scratch: How to Make Handmade Soap – A Beginners Guide and Beyond

Essential Oils and Aromatherapy - How to Use Essential Oils for Beauty, Health, and Spirituality

Little House Search – A Puzzle Book and Tour of the Works of Laura Ingalls Wilder

The Use of Magical Oils in Hoodoo, Prayer, and Spellwork

Papa Gee's Hoodoo Herbal - The Magic of Herbs, Roots, and Minerals in the Hoodoo Tradition

The Stranger in the Cup – How to Read Your Luck and Fate in the Tea Leaves by Gregory Lee White and Catherine Yronwode

How to Use Amulets, Charms, and Talismans in the Hoodoo and Conjure Tradition
by Catherine Yronwode and Gregory Lee White

Lenormand Basics – How to Read Lenormand Cards for Beginners

Casting Love Spells – Rituals of Love, Passion, and Attraction

INTRODUCTION

It is easier to reverse a hex or protect yourself from a dark spell when you know what goes into casting one. I can tell you that whenever I schedule classes in our store, my hexing class sells out in the first two days. Once, so many disappointed people couldn't get a ticket that I had to teach an encore class one hour after the first one ended. Why is that? What makes us so fascinated with the dark side of magic? Something is alluring about exploring the darker side of life because it's been depicted as forbidden and off-limits. What is beneath the surface, odd and prohibited, is something that thrills us and makes us want to know more.

Because every one of us has a dark side that we don't show to polite society. Even if you're intrigued by the idea of evil, it doesn't make you a bad person. In fact, having a thorough understanding of wickedness can be a virtue since it allows us to recognize evil more quickly and take action against it when it arises. This book will explore the craft of casting dark spells and curses from many different magical traditions, including Hoodoo, witchcraft, and other forms of folk magic. Once we have a good understanding of hexing, we will cover how to unhex and some of the tools you'll need to pull it off.

Together, we will explore how curses have worked their way into people's worlds from every walk of life, from kings to movie stars, even down to our favorite fairy tales. Grab your black candles and let's go!

DEDICATION

For my good friend, Catherine Yronwode, who taught me to be a better editor and publisher which, in turn, has made me a better writer.

ACKNOWLEDGEMENTS

Love and thanks to everyone who, through their enthusiasm on the topic, encouraged me to dive in and finally write this book.

A big thanks to my magickal friends who contributed some of their own spells. I have listed them below:
Carolina Dean
Jake Sloan

The Björketorp Runestone

WHAT IS A HEX?

It takes skill, dedication, and a little bit of hate to curse someone. It has been a part of human culture for as long as there has been a belief in the supernatural, gods, and magic. The technique of weaving dark magic is so deeply embedded in human nature that it is still carried out today in various civilizations worldwide. As humans, we crave justice when we have been wronged. When the system does not offer that justice, some turn to magic to get results.

What exactly is a curse? It is a request for bad luck to fall on someone or something, which is brought about by relying on supernatural powers. The most common type of curse is a curse placed on a person. It is designed to cast a pall over their endeavors and snuff out their enthusiasm. Nothing goes right in the world. When they seem to be getting ahead, they are knocked back down. This conjured up negative energy is directly transferred to someone (your target) in order to cause them harm. How? Written or spoken, the spell can be cast with simple words or an elaborate ritual. It depends on the situation and the creativity of the spell caster.

A curse's effect is determined by the person who casts it and the reason for doing so. The methods behind curses vary from country to country. Still, they always have one thing in common: to enforce laws and beliefs, to teach a moral lesson, to harass an enemy, or to safeguard sacred items and locations. A curse transforms speech into action, altering the energy and state of affairs in which individuals live their lives. A good example of what I mean by this is the phrase, "I now pronounce you husband and wife," which immediately affects the social status of a newlywed couple. As soon as a person speaks the correct words with authority or magical skill, the transformation occurs in a matter of seconds.

When you cast a spell, it is essential to acknowledge that you are the source of the magic. All the power that you will ever need is already within you. The magic is created by your desire, intention, faith in yourself, and the spell you plan to cast. Magic will not work unless you have a strong desire to create what you want. If you cast a spell without passion or emotion, very little magic will be infused into the spell, and chances are it will not succeed. You must pour loving feelings into the work if you are casting a love spell. For baneful magic, lighting a candle and walking away will not do the trick. Yell at the candle. Insult it. Spit in its "face." Muster up all that anger that made you want to hex someone in the first place and hold it at a controlled level while you go about your work.

So, what is the difference between a Jinx, a Hex, and a Curse? While they are all part of the same type of magical practice known as baneful magic, some people may give you different definitions according to their geographic region, culture, or religion. But for the most part, the main difference between these three things is their severity. A jinx could be considered the mildest of the three and is meant to bring on bad luck and misfortunes that may fade away over time. A hex has a bit more strength to it than a jinx. It is believed to last for a more extended period, sometimes indefinitely, until the victim takes action to have it removed. The curse would be the strongest of the three and is often meant to last a lifetime to affect a single person, an entire family, or generations of a family.

In the Hoodoo tradition, the term used would be "crossed conditions." Its origins are African and based on foot track magic using a quincunx pattern - five points in a cross shape, four of which form squares or rectangles and the fifth at the center. To give you a visual, this arrangement of five units is found on the five-spot on six-sided dice, playing cards, and dominoes. A quincunx is often used in Hoodoo as a sort of "artificial crossroads" and can be created inside a room in the house. The quincunx is generally used for scaling and fixing spells in place. So, when someone steps into the magically-charged five-spot pattern, they become cursed. Over time "crossed conditions" came to mean that someone was under the influence of a baneful spell.

PERSON, PLACE, OR OBJECT?
Curses and hexes are delivered in three different ways: on a person or group of people to bring on torment, on a place so that misfortune surrounds an area, or on an object that will transfer its curse to those who possess or interact with the object.

PEOPLE
Curses placed on a person are usually for revenge or justice because the person casting the spell has been wronged in some way. It could be revenge for murder, rape, theft, rejection, being cheated on - anything that caused pain to the spell caster. The

curse of Cain (sometimes known as the mark of Cain) in Christianity and Judaism refers to Biblical passages in Genesis where God declared that Cain, Adam and Eve's firstborn son, was cursed for murdering his brother and placed a mark on him to warn others that killing Cain would provoke God's vengeance seven times over. When God confronted Cain about Abel's death, God cursed him, saying: *"What have you done? Listen! Your brother's blood cries out to me from the ground. Now you are under a curse and driven from the ground, which opened its mouth to receive your brother's blood from your hand. When you work the ground, it will no longer yield its crops for you. You will be a restless wanderer on the earth."* (Gen. 4:10–12).

PLACES

Curses are usually placed on a specific area such as a building, a parcel of land, or a sacred space to protect them. For example, to protect the tomb's contents, we have the mummy's curse, sometimes known as the pharaoh's curse, which is said to be put on anybody who disturbs the mummy of an ancient Egyptian, particularly a pharaoh. This curse brings bad luck, disease, or death to those who bear it. Places may also be cursed when the land is stolen or something tragic occurs there. The Saco River in Maine is a site of death in American folklore. In the late 1600s, Squando, a prominent member of the Sokokis tribe, is said to have lost his wife and child in the river when they were drowned at the hands of colonial immigrants. As a kind of retaliation, Squando cursed the river, predicting that it would take three lives every year afterward. According to the New England Historical Society, the curse was allegedly broken in 1947.

OBJECTS

A cursed object has been charmed with the ability to hold a curse. It is attached to a spell, just like any other charmed object, except it emits negative energy. An object can be cursed to keep others from stealing it, or if they do, it will bring them misfortune or sorrow until it is restored to its owner. Cursed items are usually thought to have been robbed from a sanctuary or stolen from their lawful owners. These are considered protective curses, placed on a person or thing for their own protection; the curse is often inscribed on the protected object. They're like sleeping curses in that they won't be aroused unless someone tries to harm the protected object. Protective curses are similar to protective charms and amulets, but they vary in that they are intended to make an evildoer's own evil return on the sinner rather than suffocate the evil itself. The Hope Diamond is said to be blighted with such a curse, bringing bad luck to its possessor. The legends about why these objects are cursed differ, but they are frequently thought to bring bad luck or cause strange events when they are present.

THE ANCESTRAL CURSE

In essence, ancestral curses are curses that begin with a single family member and spread through the generations, affecting the lives of future generations as well. As it trickles down through the family tree, a single curse can cause them to lose everything, from their health to their finances to their social position. Several members of the same family may be affected by the same catastrophe simultaneously.

Ancestral curses are usually an open topic among family members where everybody knows about it. They retell how the great-grandfather cheated someone out of the land and ended up with a nasty curse placed on him - and the rest of them. That same story is passed down from generation to generation as an explanation for all the family's problems.

Ancestral curses are harder to break because they are so ingrained into an entire family's belief system. It is like an outsider coming in and breaking a family tradition - even though they all want it gone, it has always been there as a part of their unique story. You would assume that when enough time has passed, and the cursed person is deceased as well as the one who cast the curse, it would all be over. In my experience, that is usually true, to some degree. The brunt of the spell begins to whittle away. But the family's belief in the spell fuels it and keeps it going. Their great grandpa has doomed them all, so they go out into the world expecting to find misfortune and trouble, and, in kind, misfortune and trouble find them.

But let us entertain the idea that it is genuine and the family's opinion about the curse has nothing to do with perpetuating it. How do we get rid of it? Coming together as a family at one time, all united in battle, is an essential factor. Start with a cleansing of the person who was initially cursed. It should begin with a spiritual cleansing bath if they are still living. If they have already passed, the family should go together to the graveyard and pour hyssop tea on the grave, followed by cleansing the area with smoke and leaving a protective amulet on the headstone. Doing it together as a family is important, with everyone participating in the rituals, praying with locked hands, and blessing the amulet. From there, I would suggest they each go to their own homes and repeat the process of the spiritual bath, cleansing smoke, prayer, and protection, with all of them performing it at the same time on the same day. Planning a happy family gathering for the following day would make for a great ending.

BANEFUL OR COERCIVE OILS

When it comes to performing magic, what is considered baneful is in the eye of the beholder. Here is a list of some of the oils that can be used in dark, coercive, and controlling spells. Personally, I wouldn't consider all of them baneful because they can be used for small tricks and slight infractions. Do As I Say, for example, might be used to get your lazy teenager to clean their room and keep it that way. I wouldn't call that very dark, would you? Uncross & Reverse, to me, would be defensive magic. They started the trouble - you're just getting the hex off you and returning to sender. But some people believe that any spell that interferes with another's free will is harmful. You have to make your own call, depending on your circumstances.

- Bend Over
- Binding
- Boss Control
- Breakup
- Command
- Confusion
- Controlling
- Crossing
- Damnation
- Dark Arts
- Destroy Everything
- Do As I Say
- Dominate
- Double Cross
- D.U.M.E.
- Hot Foot
- Intranquil Spirit
- Revenge
- Reversing
- Roadblock
- Separate
- Tongue Tied
- Uncross & Reverse
- Upper Hand

CURSES AROUND THE WORLD

GREECE
Before the Olympics began, the greatest athletes in Greece would assemble before a statue of Zeus Horkios, the god of oaths. In a magical ceremony that was said to draw down the power of the gods, priests would slaughter a pig and lay the freshly cut meat at the feet of the statue.

The athletes would have to make an oath to the god of lightning not to employ foul play, bribe judges, undermine their opponents, and, most importantly, they would not use black magic to win.

However, the oath itself was bound in the dark arts. A stone tablet stood before them, warning that anyone who disobeyed his word would be cursed. It enjoined Zeus to exact his dreadful retribution on them. The athletes were assured that Zeus would smite them into ashes if a man were caught using curses and hexes to win. Some Olympic participants used the dark arts despite the threat of Zeus's wrath looming above them. Most Greeks believed in the value of praying to a dark god to gain victory. Athletes' training and dedication significantly impacted their success, but they believed that the gods decided victors and losers.

SWEDEN
The Björketorp Runestone is a monolith that is one of Sweden's greatest riddles (Pronounced Bee-york-kuh-torp). The almost 14-foot (4.2-meter) stone is found in Blekinge, Sweden, where it forms a stone

circle with two other blank menhirs and numerous other single stones. It's covered in Runes, a Proto-Norse language that contains an ominous warning regarding the stone. On one side of the stone, the inscription reads: "I, master of the runes, conceal here runes of power. Incessantly plagued by maleficence, doomed to insidious death, is he who breaks this monument." In other words, anyone who messes with this stone is in for a lot of trouble!

Scholars can't agree on what the runestone's purpose is. It's been speculated that the runestone is a burial, and the curse is meant to keep it safe. However, archaeological investigations in 1914 revealed no findings, either near the runestone or within the stone circle. It has been proposed that the runestone is a type of memorial marker instead of a gravesite.

CURSING TABLETS

Before we continue traveling the world, it is essential to explain cursing tablets since so many have been found in so many locations. Also known as defixiones, a curse tablet is a tiny tablet from the Greco-Roman era with a curse engraved on it. The terms "pierce" and "bind" come from Greek and Latin, respectively. The tablets were used to compel the gods and spirits to carry out wrathful revenge on the target. They're sometimes seen accompanied by miniature dolls or figurines with nails driven through them. Curse tablets might also include hair or clothing from the target. This was considered a means to give them power by incorporating the person's vital essence. We will discuss this more in the section on personal concerns.

Curse tablets are usually made of very thin lead sheets with the writing carved on them in small characters. The tablets were rolled, folded, or punctured with nails before being buried in graves or tombs, thrown into wells or ponds, isolated in underground sanctuaries, or attached to temple walls. People of all social statuses utilized them, and even though dark magic was frowned upon, professional spell casters could be hired to make you a curse tablet. During elections, wealthy politicians would curse their political opponents or the opposition party. Working-class people might curse robbers, murderers, or opponents of their favorite chariot racing team. Cursing tablets remained in fashion until around the 4th century, when they slowly began to fade out of style.

MESOPOTAMIA

Curse tablets were used by the ancient Egyptians, Mesopotamians, Greeks, Romans, Persians, Jews, Christians, Gauls, and Britons to pacify "unquiet" tombs and summon the demons of the underworld to cause havoc.

Inscribed on a bowl is an ancient Mesopotamian curse that petitions that the victim's "tongue may dry up in his mouth...that his legs may dry up, that sulfur and fire may burn him, that his body may be struck by scalding water, that he may be estranged, and disturbed in the eyes of all who see him, and that he may be banned, broken, lost, finished, vanquished, and that he may die, and that a flame may seize him." Pretty severe.

Various curses were written on books in a library collection in Ninevah, Mesopotamia. "Whoever shall carry off this tablet, or shall inscribe his name beside mine on it, may Ashur and Belit overcome him in rage and indignation, and may they ruin his name and posterity in the country," says one sentence. A curse was revealed in the second tomb discovered under the Nimrud Palace, threatening the person who opened the burial of Queen Yaba (wife of strong Tiglthpilese II (744-727 B.C.) with eternal hunger and restlessness.

INDIA

In 1612, Alamelamma, the wife of King Tirumalaraja, the ruler of the Vijayanagar Empire, is said to have laid a curse on the Wadiyars, the incoming royal family. When her jewels were being seized on the orders of the Wodeyar ruler, she allegedly hurried over to a rock overlooking the Kaveri river and swore, "May Talakadu become a barren area, Malangi turn into a whirlpool, and may Mysore rulers never beget offspring." She then jumped to her death. For the past 400 years, the Wadiyar dynasty has not had any offspring for alternate generations. As a result, children adopted through distant relatives must ascend to the throne. Whirlpools are steadily degrading the Mysore district. In repentance, a gold statue of Alamelamma was erected in the palace and revered as a deity. A strand of her hair was saved and kept in a box. The royal family still worships Alamelamma's idol, and, to this day, it is still found within the Mysore Palace.

BRITAIN

The Bath curse tablets are a group of around 130 Roman-era curse tablets (or defixiones in Latin) unearthed in the English city of Bath in 1979/1980. The written phrases carved on the Bath curse tablets were addressed to the goddess Sulis, who had the authority to identify the thief and impose retribution. The tablets were created as part of a rite to the goddess known as a "prayer for justice," which mixed elements of magic and religion. The goal of the prayer was not for the perpetrator to be punished in any way. It served as a warning that the thief would be punished if the things were not returned. The victim would have to first present the object to the deity in order for the curse to work, therefore making it a theft from Sulis herself.

The inscriptions are primarily in British Latin*. Two of the inscriptions are not in Latin, but they utilize the Roman alphabet and might be in a British Celtic language. Thefts of personal belongings from baths, such as jewelry, gemstones, money, household items, and especially clothes, were commonplace. "...so long as someone, whether slave or free, remains silent or knows anything about it, he may be accursed in his blood, eyes, and every limb, and even have all his intestines eaten away completely if he has stolen the ring or been privy to the crime," according to one curse.

While there are a few basic motifs in practically every known historical curse - that the victim should suffer, have no progeny, or be wretched after death - how these curses have been used, as you can see from the examples above, were very similar to each other.

*British Latin or British Vulgar Latin was the Vulgar Latin spoken in Great Britain in the Roman and sub-Roman periods.

Examples of Cursing Tablets. The bottom example is over 1600 years old and was carved onto lead, cursing a Roman senator named Fistus. "Crush, kill Fistus the senator," part of the curse reads, "May Fistus dilute, languish, sink and may all his limbs dissolve …"

FAMOUS CURSES

Here we will explore some of the more famous curses and hexes that affected everyone from kings to presidents, baseball players, brides, and even movie stars. When it comes to curses, you will find that no one is spared, despite rank or station.

THE BASANO VASE

The Basano Vase is a 15th-century silver vase presented to an Italian bride on her wedding day. However, she didn't make it to the altar since she was murdered that night while holding the vase. It was passed down her family line from there, but whoever got their hands on it is reported to have died soon afterward. The vase was packed away after untold deaths in the family and was left untouched until 1988. A piece of paper with the words "Beware...this vase brings death" was attached to the vase. The vase was reintroduced into circulation after selling for 4 million lira. The initial buyer, a pharmacist, allegedly possessed the vase for three months before he died under strange circumstances. The next owner, a 37-year-old surgeon, died two months later. The vase was re-sold to an archaeologist who prized it as a stunning example of high-renaissance craftsmanship. He passed just three months after acquiring the vase for his collection. The local police attempted to donate the vase to several museums, but the tale of the curse always deterred them. It was held in police custody for a while before disappearing. It is rumored that the police took it out to a field and buried it so that it would not be discovered again.

RUDOLPH VALENTINO'S RING

Rudolph Valentino, the handsome silent film star of the 1920s, discovered the item, known as the Destiny Ring, at a San Francisco boutique. The shopkeeper allegedly informed him that the ring was cursed and that he had no intention of selling it. Valentino was unconcerned, and after coaxing the boutique owner, he purchased it anyway. When Valentino died, it was given to his sweetheart, Pola Negri, a promising actress. That is until she received the ring. From there, her career took a turn for the worst, and her health began to fail. After realizing it may genuinely be cursed, she gave the ring to an acquaintance, Russ Columbo. Columbo was killed in a strange accident involving a rifle that he and a friend were handling. It then went to a man named Joe Casino, who was killed by a speeding car. The ring then made its way to Casino's brother. But before its curse could affect him, it was stolen by a robber named James Willis. Willis was shot by police as soon as they arrived on the scene. After that, the ring appears to have taken one more person and then vanished from history.

THE DELHI PURPLE SAPPHIRE

During the Mutiny of 1857, a British soldier is said to have stolen a mysterious stone from the Temple of Indra (the Hindu deity of war and weather) in Kanpur, India. Also known as 'the gem of sorrow,' this enchanted stone brings misery, misfortune, and terrible sadness. Colonel W. Ferris, a Bengal Cavalryman, removed what he thought was a purple sapphire from the shrine before leaving India. After that, he returned to his family. Ferris began to endure a series of financial disasters when he returned to England, bringing the family to the verge of bankruptcy. When the rest of his family began to suffer from serious ailments, he shifted his attention to the stone. When he gave the stone to a family friend who mysteriously committed suicide, his worries were verified.

In 1890, the stone was presented to Edward Heron-Allen, a scientist and writer. Soon after obtaining the gem, Edward lost all sense of reason and blamed a series of negative events on the stone's curse. In 1902, Heron-Allen reluctantly consented to let a friend borrow the Delhi Sapphire. A succession of misfortunes happened to the friend almost immediately. He returned the jewel to Edward, who began experiencing troubles once again. He threw the stone into Regent's Canal out of frustration. Edward assumed he had finally rid himself of the gem. But it was excavated from the canal and sent to a local jeweler a few months later. The jeweler recognized the stone right away as the one he had set for Heron-Allen with two amethyst scarab beetles and the symbols of the zodiac. So, he returned it. When a friend asked to borrow it many years later, Heron-Allen gave it out once more. This time, the unlucky receiver was a professional vocalist who could never sing again after wearing the cursed jewel.

The Delhi Purple sapphire, according to Heron-Allen, is "accursed and tainted with the blood and disgrace of everyone who has ever had it." He kept it hidden in seven boxes, surrounded it with good luck charms, and placed it in his bank vault. Heron-Allen died in 1944. Despite Heron-Allen's insistence that the box not be opened for 33 years after his death, his daughter delivered it to the Natural History Museum as soon as she could. There it sat until 1972, languishing in a drawer until curator Peter Tandy unearthed the sapphire and the unusual letter that came with it, chronicling the stone's specific tales of misery. "Do anything you want with this package, whoever opens it." However, my recommendation is to toss it into the sea." The Delhi Purple sapphire is now permanently on exhibit in the Vault Collection of London's Natural History Museum.

THE HOPE DIAMOND

The Hope Diamond, a magnificent blue diamond measuring over 45 carats, is one of the world's most remarkable diamonds. The stone, which is around the size of a walnut, is estimated at a quarter of a billion dollars. But the curse that goes along with it is another story. Its origins are believed to be in India, where it rested on the brow (some say the eye) of a Hindu temple deity statue. When priests discovered the diamond was missing, they placed a curse on whoever had stolen it. The thief is suspected of being Jean-Baptiste Tavernier, who either stole it himself or bribed another to steal it for him. Some reports say he died of a raging fever soon after returning from India, while others say he lived until the age of 84. Tavernier sold the diamond and 14 other large diamonds and numerous lesser ones to King Louis XIV of France in 1668. Sieur Pitau, the court jeweler, recut the stone in 1673. The stone became known as the "Blue Diamond of the Crown" or the "French Blue." It was gold-plated and hung on a ribbon around the king's neck on ceremonial occasions.

The French Blue was finally passed down to Louis XVI and Marie Antoinette. By 1793, their heads had rolled, and all of their children but one had perished. The French Blue vanished during the turmoil of the French Revolution. It ultimately resurfaced as a 45.52-carat stone that had been recut to avoid detection.

Henry Thomas Hope bought the diamond in 1839 and named it for himself. Despite the favorable title, his heirs were plagued by bad luck and sold the estate to pay off gambling debts. Hendrik Fals, the son of Dutch jeweler Wilhelm Fals, killed his father and stole the diamond after recutting it again. Hendrik later took his own life. Another owner, Greek trader Simon Maoncharides, was killed together with his wife and son after driving off a cliff. By the 20th century, the diamond was now owned by the famous jeweler Pierre Cartier, who sold it to the gold-mine heiress Evelyn Walsh McLean. While in her possession, McLean suffered through the death of her nine-year-old son, her husband left her for another woman, she spent time in a mental institution, and lost her entire fortune.

In 1949, the Hope Diamond and McLean's entire estate jewelry collection were bought by Harry

Winston. The stone traveled the world for ten years as part of The Court of Jewels show, which featured other valuable jewels. Winston decided to present the diamond to the Smithsonian Institute and, instead of hiring a proper courier, shipped the jewel by first-class mail. The mailman who delivered the parcel, James Todd, would add to the jewel's notoriety. He said his leg was crushed in a car accident, and his house burned to the ground.

THE CURSE OF TIPPECANOE

Tecumseh's Curse, also known as the Tippecanoe Curse, resulted from a feud between US President William Henry Harrison and Shawnee Indigenous leader Tecumseh in 1809. Governor of the Indian Territory, William Henry Harrison, was tasked with confronting Tecumseh and his band of warriors. The Battle of Tippecanoe was the name given to the battle. The song-turned-slogan "Tippecanoe and Tyler Too!" became well-known during Harrison's successful presidential campaign. When the Shawnee were defeated, Tecumseh's brother, Tenskwatawa, cast a curse on Harrison and all future Presidents, declaring that they would die in office in a cursed year divisible by twenty. Some think the curse is to blame for Harrison's death in office and that of every subsequent president until Kennedy, who was elected in a year ending in zero. Others say the curse was cast by Tecumseh himself. The presidents elected in such years from 1840 to 1960 died in office: William Henry Harrison (1840), Abraham Lincoln (1860), James A. Garfield (1880), William McKinley (1900), Warren G. Harding (1920), Franklin D. Roosevelt (1940) and John F. Kennedy (1960). The curse seems to have been broken with the 1980 shooting of Ronald Reagan, who survived.

CURSE OF THE BILLY GOAT

The Billy Goat Curse was a sports curse allegedly cast on the Chicago Cubs Major League Baseball team by Billy Goat Tavern owner William Sianis in 1945. From 1945 until 2016, the curse lasted 71 years. Sianis' pet goat, Murphy, upset other spectators during Game 4 of the 1945 World Series at Wrigley Field, and the two were ordered to leave. Outraged, Sianis allegedly said, "Those Cubs, they ain't going to win no more," implying that the Cubs will never win the National League pennant again. The Cubs were defeated in the 1945 World Series by the Detroit Tigers, and they did not win another World Series until 2016. The last time the Cubs won the World Series was in 1908. For 71 years, the Cubs did not play in the World Series after the incident with Sianis and Murphy, until finally, the "curse" was broken on the 46th anniversary of William Sianis's death when they defeated the Los Angeles Dodgers 5–0 in game 6 of the 2016 National League Championship Series to win the NL pennant.

THE CURSE OF THE PHARAOHS - KING TUT

King Tut's Curse is one of the world's most renowned curses. Since the discovery of King Tutankhamun's tomb in Egypt's Valley of the Kings, legends have spread that anybody who attempted to desecrate the child king's final resting place would be cursed. In the Valley of the Kings, across the Nile from Luxor in Egypt, British archaeologist Howard Carter found the tomb of Pharaoh Tutankhamun, who died in 1323

BC at the age of roughly 18, in late 1922. From the 16th to the 11th century BC, pharaohs were buried there. Tutankhamun's tomb was the first to be found nearly fully undamaged, despite most of the tombs having been robbed since ancient times. Carter and his team were joined by the 5th Earl of Carnarvon, an amateur Egyptologist who was funding the project. As they entered the burial chambers, they discovered the young pharaoh's mummified body and a wealth of religious objects, wall paintings, inscriptions, and equipment he would need in the afterlife.

Lord Carnarvon died in Cairo at 56, and the city's lights went out, setting off a flurry of conjecture. According to Arthur Conan Doyle, Carnarvon's death might have been caused by an 'evil elemental' ghost conjured by priests to preserve the mummy. The actual cause was blood poisoning, a combination of a mosquito bite and a cut from shaving that became infected. He is buried at Highclere Castle (filming location for Downton Abbey), where some Egyptian artifacts are still displayed.

Although no curse had been discovered in the tomb, the deaths of different members of Carter's crew and real or imagined visitors to the site throughout the years kept the narrative alive, especially in cases of death by violence or in unusual circumstances. Prince Ali Kamel Fahmy Bey of Egypt, who was assassinated in Cairo in 1923 by his wife; Sir Archibald Douglas Reid, who allegedly X-rayed the mummy and died mysteriously in 1924; Sir Lee Stack, the governor-general of Sudan, who was assassinated in Cairo in 1924; Arthur Mace of Carter's excavation team, said to have died of arsenic poisoning in 1928; and Carter's secretary Richard Bethell found smothered in his sleep.

THE EVIL EYE

The belief in the evil eye has its roots in the Middle East and the Mediterranean cultures, where it can either result from envy or, more rarely, a malicious curse. The best way to describe it would be to imagine poison darts of magic coming from one person's eyes and into their target, resulting in misery and misfortune. The evil eye can be warded off by wearing a protective object composed of dark blue circular glass with a white circle surrounding a black dot in the center, which resembles the eye's pupil. Protection for the eyes comes in a variety of shapes and sizes. It appeared on Chalcidian drinking containers known as 'eye-cups' as far back as the 6th century BC as a sort of apotropaic magic (the power to reject or deflect the evil eye). Since glass beads didn't appear until sometime around 1500 BC, the evil eye symbol was mainly found on items made of ceramic or clay. There is a tradition of testing for the curse where a single drop of olive oil is placed into a vessel of holy water. If the droplet floats, no evil eye is present.

INTRANQUIL SPIRIT

The Intranquil Spirit refers to a spirit that travels restlessly but cannot find a home or resting place. The Intranquil Spirit's origins and why it's called that are unknown, although it is believed to have originated in Mexico. It is not uncommon to call upon verbal love charms to dominate an ex-lover. It is thought that the Intranquil Spirit cannot reach Heaven but hasn't transgressed enough to be sentenced to Hell. So, it is left to wander the Earth, much like a form of purgatory found in Catholicism. While those of European ancestry think of ghosts locked into a specific place such as a house or a plot of land, the concept is different in Mexico, where they believe a spirit can move about more freely. These spirits are called upon to remedy love matters, especially to bring back a lover who has left and refuses to return. The Intranquil Spirit is summoned to torment the ex and even bring them to the brink of madness, if necessary, to force them to come back to the relationship. It doesn't sound like a very loving act, does it?

CURSES AS A PLOT DEVICE

Curses have been used in literature, theater, and fairy tales for hundreds of years. They are the theme of many movies and television programs and can even be found in gaming. When they are utilized as a plot device, they involve one character casting a curse or hex on another, which moves the story forward as the recipient of the curse must battle or deal with its effects.

FAIRY TALES

Fairy tales thrive on curses. But the original versions of your favorite fairytales might be much darker than you would ever imagine, with cannibalism, child abuse, rape, and graphic violence stories.

SLEEPING BEAUTY

This dark tale has gone through many incarnations over the years and is thought to have first been told around 1330. Early versions tell how an evil fairy cursed the princess to fall into a deep sleep after pricking her finger on a piece of flax. One version mentions seven fairies, one who was not invited because she had been locked in a tower for many years and presumed dead. When she shows up at the christening, she bestows the gift of a curse. The Grimm fairytale version replaced the flax with the spindle of a spinning wheel. But those early versions include how a wandering king came across the sleeping girl, raped her while she still slept, and impregnated her with twins. Charming. It is not until she gives birth that one of the babies brings out the flax that initially put her to sleep, thus awakening her.

However, we can see how the story of a simple kiss awakening her came to be - it was a much-needed, G-rated interpretation of events.

Illustration from an older version of Sleeping Beauty

SNOW WHITE

The original story was published in 1812 by the Brothers Grimm and featured many of the same elements we know today: the vain stepmother, the magic mirror, the poisoned apple, and the seven dwarves (although the dwarves were nameless in the original story.) We are familiar with the evil Queen wanting the Huntsman to bring her Snow White's heart in the modern telling. Initially, she requested her lungs and liver so that the Queen could eat them. When she finds out the Huntsman didn't do the job, the Queen sets out to kill Snow White herself. Disguised, she sells Snow a bodice and laces her up so tightly that she collapses but is revived by the dwarves. The second assassination attempt is with a poison-tipped comb, but the dwarves wake her again. The poisoned apple finally does the trick, and the dwarves rest her in a glass coffin.

A prince comes across the supposedly dead Snow White lying in her glass casket during a hunting trip. After hearing Snow White's narrative from the Seven Dwarfs, the prince is permitted to take her body to his father's castle, a more appropriate resting place. Suddenly, one of the prince's servants falls and loses his footing while transporting Snow White. This miraculously resurrects Snow White by dislodging a chunk of poisoned apple from her throat. Of course, they fall in love and plan to wed. The Queen is invited to Snow White's wedding, where the guests heat a pair of iron shoes over a fire and force her to wear them and dance in torment until she dies.

Both the stories of Sleeping Beauty and Snow White traditionally ended their curses with a magical kiss - not found in either original version of the stories. But what is interesting is the vehicle in which the curses were cast. Neither was simply by chanting a spell or magical words. They both included cursed objects, which brought about the deep sleep of these two maidens. Neither the flax (later spinning wheel) nor the apple caused permanent death - just a cursed, deep sleep. So, you might say that if the goal were to kill them, the spell caster didn't do a very good job. But, as a plot device, it makes sense. If you kill off your leading lady right away in your story, and she's dead for good, that doesn't make for much of a plot.

LITERATURE

We've been telling stories with hexes and curses for as long as stories have been told, filled with bad luck, punishments, and redemption. But whatever the reason they were cast, these curses deliver precisely what we humans crave in literature and our everyday lives: clear causes for disastrous consequences and explanations for the terrifying and irrational. They are lessons in cause and effect.

THE HOUSE OF THE SEVEN GABLES

Nathaniel Hawthorne's novel The House of the Seven Gables follows the generations of a Puritan family and the curse that follows them. The Pyncheons are a well-respected family in their little Massachusetts town, but their past is filled with mysteries, inexplicable deaths, and a dying man's curse. Colonel Pyncheon is a wealthy and influential Puritan from Salem, Massachusetts. He has one ambition: to bequeath his descendants a magnificent home. After much hunting, he finally discovers the perfect spot for his house, adjacent to a freshwater spring. But there's a snag. Matthew Maule, a poor man, owns the property. Maule refuses to sell Colonel Pyncheon his land since he has recently cleared and tilled it. Colonel Pyncheon, on the other hand, is patient. Pyncheon saw his opportunity when witchcraft mania swept Salem in 1692. He accuses Maule of witchcraft, and Maule is hanged as a result.

Maule curses Pyncheon before dying, warning him that 'God will give him blood to drink.'

Pyncheon begins construction on a large residence, which he names the House of the Seven Gables, as soon as he obtains Maule's land. However, Matthew Maule's curse reappears on the day of Colonel Pyncheon's housewarming party. Pyncheon is discovered dead, his neck covered in blood. The curse has begun. And so the story continues with the descendants of Colonel Pyncheon being affected by the curse.

THE BOOK OF SPECULATION

In this novel by Erika Swyler, we have Simon and Enola Watson, who are from a line of breath-holding carnival mermaids. Still, each generation of Watson women suddenly drowns on the same day every year. In this novel, the plot is about the investigation of a curse with Simon trying to find out the source of it to attempt to end it. The clues to the curse of July 24th are strange ecological events, a mysterious ancient book, and a collapsing house. I will tell you that the story deals with a cursed object causing the problem, but not being an author who enjoys publishing spoilers, you will have to read it to find out what that object is. It may not be the one you thought.

THE BOY WHO LOST HIS FACE

In this 1989 young adult novel by Louis Sachar, we are introduced to the main character, David, a young boy in middle school. His friend, Scott, wants to hang out with the cool kids, but David isn't quite cool enough to be accepted into the group. When the boys decide to take an elderly lady's cane, the old woman casts a curse with David as the target. Everything goes wrong suddenly: David smashes his parents' bedroom window, his fly is never zipped, his pants come down, and he pours flour all over the place. Meanwhile, his "friends" mock him and exclude him from their social circles. While you'll have to read the book to find out what happens, this is an excellent example of a curse cast by using nothing but words. Or do the words create a self-fulfilling curse?

MOVIES

Hollywood and television have used curses and hexes in their plot too many times to count. But here are my two favorite examples, each one using a different type of curse.

PRACTICAL MAGIC

The Owens family curse is one of the fundamental conflicts in the film. The first thing viewers learn about Maria Owens is that she cursed her family (accidentally), resulting in a generational curse that any man who dared to love an Owens woman would die. Her original intention was to call a spell on herself so that she would not feel the pain of love loss. But, over time, it caused her to turn bitter and the spell transformed into a curse. When Sally and Gillian's father dies when they are only children, we see the curse in action. Their mother passes away due to a broken heart, and the two girls are forced to live with their aunts. The curse reappears several years later, this time with Sally's husband, who also succumbs to the curse and is hit by a truck. The elimination of the curse was one of the many difficulties remedied after the ritual that took care of Jimmy.

There is no curse in Alice Hoffman's book *Practical Magic*. Sally and Gillian's parents, as well as Sally's husband, do pass away. (In the book, he is hit by a car full of teenagers when he steps off the curb.) However, none of these fatalities have anything to do with the curse. These deaths are solely to drive the plot forward.

DRAG ME TO HELL

Christine Brown works as a loan officer at a bank, and she is competing for an assistant manager position with a coworker. Because her boss thinks she is incapable of making hard decisions, she declines a time extension on a loan to an elderly woman, Mrs. Ganush, who is facing foreclosure and the loss of her home. In vengeance, the elderly woman casts a curse on her, which she later discovers will result in her being dragged to hell after three days of being tormented by a Lamia demon. (In mythology, a Lamia is a demon who devours children.) She eventually turns to a psychic who has had experience with a Lamia to try and exorcise the demon. Here we have a curse that calls upon an outside force, a demon, to carry out its wrath, a similar, but more serious, scenario to calling upon an Intranquil Spirit.

Whether the curse appears in books, television, the theater, movies, or beloved fairy tales, any good fiction writer will appreciate the one thing they have to offer - they provide the characters with a conflict that seems impossible to hurdle. As readers and viewers, we love to be left on the edge of our seat wondering if the hero will get past trouble and get their happy ending.

HEX APPEAL

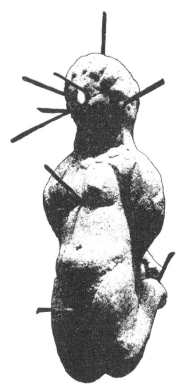

Egyptian Effigy, Circa 3rd-4th Century AD

A folded lead tablet with a magic binding spell was found in a terracotta vase containing this little clay effigy doll. With her feet tied together and her arms cuffed behind her back, the effigy is pierced with thirteen pins: one in the top of her head, one in each eye and ear, one in the solar plexus, one in the vagina, and one in each palm and sole of each foot.

The inscription in Greek reads:
"Bring me Ptolemais, the daughter of Horigenes whom Aias bore. Prevent her from eating or drinking until she arrives at my home, Sarapammon, whom Area bore, and do not allow her to experience any other men, except for me. For the rest of my life, I will keep her obedient to me by her hair, by her innards, until she does not stand aloof from me and tells me what she is thinking."

The Louvre Museum in Paris has this effigy on exhibit.

SHOULD YOU HEX SOMEONE?

The most effective curses have some element of planning to them. While there may be high emotion in a spontaneous curse that is said in anger, we don't always think clearly in those moments. This can also create a sloppy or incomplete spell. This chapter will discuss the ethics of cursing, questions to ask yourself before committing to the act, and how to protect yourself in the process.

BIND, BANISH, OR CURSE?

BINDING
Think of binding as a magical restraining order. Binding doesn't have to be a hostile act; it is frequently used to keep someone from harming themselves or others. So, with a binding, you aren't performing baneful magic against the person - it is more like proactive protection magic. In the past, binding was often used in folk magic to prevent ghosts and restless spirits from straying out of graveyards to keep them from haunting the living. Binding spells generally entail the symbolic binding, wrapping, tying, or otherwise confining an object representing the bound person - most often a doll or photograph. Other spells might have you take the effigy of your target and place it inside a box or vessel, then bind the box shut with twine or wax. In 1940, Gerald Gardner, the founder of the Gardnerian Wicca religion, met in the woods with his New Forest Coven and performed a cone of power ceremony to prevent Hitler's forces from entering the United Kingdom. In other words, they bound Hitler from

having the power to complete his mission. Whether it was because of the spell or other forces, there is no way to tell, but Hitler did not enter.

BANISHING

Banishing is often used in ceremonial magic to describe one or more rituals used to eliminate non-physical entities such as spirits or negative influences. It is performed as a precaution to rid the area of anything that might interfere with the magic that is about to be cast. Although banishing rituals are frequently done as part of larger ceremonies, they can also be performed independently. Many Wiccans perform a banishing before casting a magic circle to purify the space where the ritual or magic is about to take place. This type of banishing would probably fall more in the category of protection magic because those performing the banishing don't actually know if there is anything negative in the space, to begin with.

Smoke purification, salt, chants, prayers, sigils, stones or crystals, bells, ritual bathing, burning papers, candles, direct energy manipulation, meditation, or trance are all common ways to work banishing spells. Banishing is not only used to rid a space of negative energy but also to remove hostile or toxic people from your life. Banishing a person doesn't have to include wishing harm on them - it is simply an act of getting them to leave, to get out of your life. It would all depend on how you worded your spell or prayer. To rid yourself of someone who is abusive, and you are finding it difficult to get them to move on, adding a more baneful aspect to the spell might be necessary. Although, it doesn't have to be permanent. Many spells are worked so that bad luck and misery will continue to follow your target unless they do as you command. In other words, as long as they stay away from you and leave you alone, their world will be fine. But when they try to re-enter your life or cause trouble, the nasty stuff kicks back in.

CURSING

Since we've already covered what a curse is, let's talk about the motivations and emotions behind casting one. For me, cursing is a last resort that should be used under extreme circumstances such as revenge for rape, murder, or theft. I've seen too many people want to curse their old boyfriend because he broke up with them while, at the same time, they're saying they want him back. That doesn't make any sense to me. So, you want him even more screwed up than when he left? Yeah, that should make you a happy couple! That sort of cursing work is not justified (see next section.) Cursing someone is a commitment and bonds you to them. You are entering into a contract to spend your energy ruining their life. When you take time out of your life to pursue vengeance rather than moving on, you're squandering opportunities to improve your life and live happier moments. The person who wronged you may deserve to be punished, and that decision lies with you and you are alone. But studies have shown that seeking revenge can make us feel worse, wrapped up in dark and negative emotions that we won't let go of, and, with every day we entertain those feelings, they become more and more a part of our psyche. Giving yourself a time limit to live in the anger so that you don't wind up in the same spot years later is a good compromise. But, if your mind is made up and a curse is what you seek, you've come to the right book!

IS IT JUSTIFIED?

What does it mean for a work to be justified? Basically, the punishment should fit the crime. When someone jeopardizes your personal safety, money, marriage, home, profession, or reputation, you are typically justified in carrying out a spell against them to some level. If the work is actually justified and what you intend for them is morally balanced with what they did to you, you usually don't have to be concerned with the repercussions of performing a binding, banishment, or curse. Let me repeat once again - the punishment should fit the crime. What does that mean? It's founded on the retributive justice principle, which states that when an offender breaks the law, justice demands that they suffer as a result and that the punishment for a crime should be proportional to the crime. In my experience, if the work is not justified, then the spell has less chance of working.

Let's return to the scene with the boyfriend who broke up with you. It doesn't sound like much reason to cast a baneful spell. However, if he also slept with your sister and stole your car before leaving, that sounds like a good reason for cursing! Think of it this way - when driving, you don't get the death penalty for not using your turn signal. You also don't get a warning ticket for homicide. The dictionary definition of justified is: "having or shown to have a just, right, or reasonable basis." Just because you are hurt or angry about what someone did or said doesn't necessarily make it justifiable. It is sometimes best to take a step back from the situation before deciding how to proceed. Wait a week before casting that spell.

IS IT ETHICAL?

This is a topic I mentioned in my previous book, Casting Love Spells: Rituals of Love, Passion, and Attraction. There are two kinds of ethics: subjective ethics and objective ethics. In short, subjective ethics is based on the idea that right and wrong decisions for one person may not be so for another; it is all due to an individual's circumstances, upbringing, and cultural background. Subjective ethics are based on a person's judgment of what is right or wrong and how they would feel about doing magic if they were in the other person's place. Many people mistakenly associate ethics with their emotions. On the other hand, being ethical is not a question of going with one's gut instincts. Following one's sentiments might lead to a reluctance to do what is right. In reality, emotions regularly diverge from ethical behavior.

It is also a mistake to equate ethics with religion. Ethics refers to well-founded moral norms that dictate what humans should do, generally regarding rights, duties, societal advantages, justice, or special virtues. Of course, most religions promote high ethical standards. However, if ethics were limited to religion, it would only apply to religious individuals. Ethics apply equally to the actions of atheists as they do to devoted religious people.

Your morals and cultural background may influence your magical path. For example, many Wiccans believe in the three-fold rule, which states that whatever you put out returns back to you three times. Those regulations, however, do not apply to a Hoodoo practitioner. They would see the spell as more of a prayer to God. And if the spell fails, God has refused to fulfill their wish. This protects the spell caster from any negative consequences. Do you think of yourself as an ethical person? Will your ethics play a part in deciding whether to bind, banish, or cast a full-out curse? I'll leave you to ponder that.

GOT KARMA?

Karma is hard to define because it depends on who you ask. For example, the different schools of Hinduism have other ideas about how karma and rebirth are linked, while Buddhism and Jainism have their own karma doctrines. Some believe that your deeds, good and bad, are repaid in the next life, while others claim that repayment can occur in the life you are currently living. Basically, karma is based on the idea that every action has a consequence that will manifest in this life or in a future life. Morally good deeds will have positive effects, while cruel acts will have negative consequences.

"An experienced witch does not rely on karma. She relies on magickal justice."
— Dacha Avelin, author of *Old World Witchcraft: Pathway to Effective Magick*

Although they usually don't mention the word 'karma,' I've had many people ask, "will this come back to me?" about performing darker or negative spells. The concept is the same. If I do something bad, will it come back to haunt me? In India, there is a saying, "a person who intends ill for others brings misery for himself." In the Christian Bible, we have Galatians 6:7-8 *"Do not be deceived, God is not mocked; for whatever a man sows, that he will also reap. For he who sows to the flesh will of the flesh reap corruption, but he who sows to the Spirit will of the Spirit reap everlasting life."* There is also a command based on the words of Jesus in the Sermon on the Mount: *"All things whatsoever ye that men would do to you, do ye even so to them."* The Mosaic law contains a parallel commandment: "Whatever is hurtful to you, do not do to any other person." As already mentioned, in some Wiccan and pagan paths there is, "Ever mind the rule of three – what ye send out comes back to thee." In other words, they believe cursing another individual will risk bringing bad juju upon themselves.

White clover flowers are used for protection against evil influences

PROTECTING YOURSELF

Protection work and baneful magic should go hand-in-hand to keep the negative energy of dark spells off of you. We just talked about karma and how it may affect your next life. But there is a pressing matter you should deal with today, in this life - what if the person you cast ill will upon decides to reverse the spell and send it back to you? How dark did you go when you cast that curse, and what are your feelings about experiencing everything you wished on your magical target? These are known as 'reversing' spells or 'return to sender' spells. We make a magical condition oil in our shop called Uncross and Reverse. It is meant to be used ritually to take off crossed conditions and send them back to the person who cast it.

Reversal spells are not difficult to accomplish. So, if you are the one casting the dark spell, remember that the recipient can send it right back to you if you don't adequately protect yourself and your space. This doesn't necessarily apply to only curses or banishing. For example, if you were to perform a coercion spell to coax someone into doing something they don't want to do, they could easily send that back to you. This is known as "turning the trick."

It may seem overkill, but you should do cleansing work before and after performing cursing or baneful work. Why ahead of time? For the same reason as I described in the Pagan banishing ritual - to cleanse a space of any energies that might interfere with the work or make it go awry - or even backfire. Before your magical work, you might cleanse the area with smoke (such as burning sage or incense), sweeping, scattering with salt, or sprinkling holy water. Pray, speak, or meditate on your intentions while performing the cleansing. After your baneful work, you will want to go a little further. Cleanse the space again, then spiritually cleanse yourself. A bath including hyssop is one method. Some choose to surround themselves with a cleansing circle of smoke. Then lock down your cleansing work with protection work. (see the section towards the back of the book for cleansing and hex removal spells and rituals.)

THE PLACEBO HEX

First of all, if you haven't heard of it, what is a placebo? The dictionary definition is: "a harmless pill, medicine, or procedure prescribed more for the psychological benefit to the patient than for any physiological effect." So, how can this be applied to the topic of hexing and cursing? Curses are almost always carried out in complete secrecy without the curse's target ever knowing where it came from or who cast it. But what if you were to actually tell someone that you cursed them? Would it affect them? If they are the type of person who believes in the world of magic and that you are capable of casting a well-crafted spell, then it could affect them greatly.

Furthermore, you don't actually have to do the baneful work behind it to make it work. You only have to say you did. Sometimes the very idea that a curse has been placed on someone will cause them to create their own series of mishaps and misfortunes. Hence, the placebo effect. This psychological burden of a hex they now carry around with them creates confusion, anxiety, and worry, which can lead to bad decisions and passing up opportunities. They begin to question every little thing that goes wrong. Did the argument with the boyfriend come from the curse? Is that the reason they didn't get the job they applied for? Is that why they got a speeding ticket? It can take on a snowball effect, causing more bad luck as they become consumed with negative energy, often to the point of needing an unhexing ritual to remove what was never there in the first place.

The presence of a baneful-looking object can also work as a form of protection magic, even if no magic were performed on that object. If you have a bundle of gnarled sticks bound with twine and bones hanging over your front door, it can ward off potential thieves (if they are superstitious.) Many years ago, I had a friend who was a Buddist with a temple in his backyard. He was also a colorful character who dyed his hair jet-black and wore kimonos, even to mow the yard. While he lived in a high crime rate neighborhood, he never experienced a single problem. "They all think I'm a witch around here," he would say. "Good. Let 'em think it. Nobody messes with us." So, a rumor (that he embraced) became a form of protection magic, even though no magical spell had been performed.

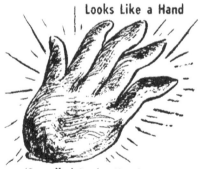

1930s advertisement for a Lucky Hand root from the Masters Supply House catalog out of New York.

LAYING TRICKS

Laying down tricks, fixing tricks, throwing down, and laying down are all terms used to describe casting spells in the Hoodoo tradition. To 'lay a trick' is to magically place down, bury, hide, or toss the spellwork in a location that is likely to be walked over. Herbs, powders, and other ingredients are placed in an area where they will come into contact with the intended target to induce a specific effect. Burying bottles, flinging powders, and hiding mojo bags are all instances of tricks, and they can be deployed in countless ways by setting them in places that your target will not only walk over, but also any objects they touch. Whatever your tradition, spells tend to work better when you use age-old knowledge and ingredients, or at the very least, include some of them in your original spells.

HOT FOOT

In Hoodoo, foot track magic is a trick in which a person's footprints are used against them to drive them away. Hot Foot Powder is the most widely-used and well-known way to carry out the magic. It's made up of herbs and minerals, with chili powder, pepper, chili flakes, and sometimes salt. Other elements like wasp's nests, sulfur, and graveyard dirt are used. It is similar to goofer dust, which is known to cause agitation and make people want to leave, although goofer dust is usually used to harm the target.

While there is no way to know, some scholars say that Hot Foot powder may not be a historical practice but rather a commercialized and misunderstood version of the traditional Walkin' Foot, a powder used in traditional African-American Hoodoo to cause a person to walk in all directions, alter the way they walked, or to make their legs tremble. The practice was influenced by West African foot track magic, in which individuals take a person's footprints and mix them with ingredients to control their movements. Traditionally, one would take the herbs, roots, and ingredients we just covered above to make a powder that was combined with a person's foot track (the dirt from a place where they walked) and sprinkled it on their shoes or in their path to 'hoodoo the person.' It is usually mixed with dirt before sprinkling onto a pathway to disguise it.

In India, it is believed that footprints left by a holy person have magical powers. Because the feet provide support for the body, it was widely believed that they also symbolized the soul. Historically, many civilizations thought that the feet were particularly vulnerable to evil energies.

One traditional Hoodoo charm is to wear ankle amulets consisting of nine pieces of Devil's Shoestring and a silver coin (usually a mercury dime) to protect from the dangers of foot-track magic. If the silver dime turned black, it indicated the presence of evil. Silver was considered magically neutral in many cultures as it would not contain or enable contamination from the spirit realm.

Some more creative ways to use hot foot powder have nothing to do with working magic on another person. Sprinkle some hot foot powder around your mailbox if you want to keep bad news away. Place some in a small red bag and keep by the phone to prevent harassing phone calls. Sprinkle on the edge of your property line to make nosy neighbors mind their own business and keep their prying eyes off your home. Spread some on your front walkway and porch to keep away thieves - especially helpful if you've had problems with porch pirates stealing your packages.

MIRROR BOX

A mirror box is an act of both revenge and justice. The entire point of the mirror box is that an enemy who has done you wrong will be forced into the box where they must forever look at themselves and what they have done. Preparing the mirror box is the first thing you will need to do. Buy a mirror in which your reflection has never been captured. Make sure not to look in it when you are crafting the box. While breaking a mirror with a hammer is traditional, you can now purchase small mirrors in craft stores. Next, you will need a small box made of wood or cardboard. It only needs to be big enough to hold what you put inside. It is best to use someone's photograph or a doll that represents them because it should be an effigy with eyes in order for them to see their reflection. Dolls don't have to be purchased, and they don't have to be big. They can be no larger than the size of your thumb and made out of clay, cloth, mud, or even by carving out a piece of cheese. Glue the mirrors inside the box on the bottom, sides, and inside the lid. Place the doll inside and sprinkle it with just a few baneful herbs and peppers (you don't want to cover up the mirrors.) You might include a petition attached to the doll or, if you used a photograph, write on the back of it stating what horrors you have in store for your enemy.

COFFIN BOX

A coffin box spell can be used the same way as a mirror box spell, providing you line the coffin with mirrors. But, traditionally, the coffin box (usually crafted so that it will fit in your hand) has a slightly different energy than a mirror box. With a mirror box, you force your target to look at themselves and what they've done. With a coffin, you are simply trapping that person for the sake of revenge, teaching a lesson, keeping them away from you (sometimes for protective reasons), or, even darker, wishing for the death of that person. Many of the same baneful herbs and spices are used in the coffin alongside items like nails, broken glass, and twine to bind up the doll or effigy you place in the coffin. Just be very clear about your motives and what you intend for your target before placing them in a casket in the ground. On the other side of the coin, some people use coffin boxes for themselves to put an end to something, bury an addiction problem, or bury their emotions for someone who is obviously not going to return the feelings.

In 1836 a group of boys went rabbit hunting on the slopes of Arthur's Seat (some claim to be the site of Camelot) in Edinburgh, Scotland. They discovered a small opening in the rock buried behind three-pointed slabs of slate in a remote area on the hill's northeast side. There were 17 small coffins hidden inside. While experts haven't ruled out witchcraft, they came to the conclusion that due to the care that was used in dressing the dolls inside the coffin and the absence of herbs or other objects, the coffins were placed there to represent loved ones that had possibly been lost at sea or died in a faraway land. Eight of these coffins have survived and are on display in Scotland's National Museum.

FREEZER SPELLS

This container spell helps to stop someone from speaking or acting against you. So, a nagging coworker can be silenced, and a stalker can be placed on hold. Freezer spells are intended to quiet or remove someone from your life. The spell's primary goal is to get someone to cease doing something that is harmful to others. This spell is commonly referred to as 'the freezer spell' or 'the icebox spell.' It's also known as 'putting them on ice.' To work a freezer spell, gather petitions and photographs, personal objects belonging to your target, and corresponding herbs, place them into a container, and then store them in the freezer. If you ever want to reverse the spell, take it out, allow it to thaw, and dispose of it. I can tell you that I, personally, have never performed a freezer spell. I've never liked the idea of trapping a hateful asshole in the same freezer where I store food I intend to eat.

LIVE THINGS INSIDE YOU

The types of curses known as 'live things inside you' fall under the category of what is known as magical poisoning. This magic uses the power of creatures like ants, spiders, worms, maggots, ticks, roaches, leeches, etc. to infect a person by magically putting them, or the sensation of them, into your target's body. Other known terms include magical 'infestation,' 'invasion,' and 'affliction.' In her 1895 essay, Alice Bacon writes: *"The conjure doctor told him that he had been conjured and that inside of him were a number of small snakes which ate up the food as fast as he ate it. Another woman who had lizards crawling in her body was obliged to eat very often to keep the lizards from eating her."* Of course, there are also instances of actual infestations, such as severe tapeworms, where the patient associated this very real medical condition with being 'hoodooed.'

WITCH BOTTLES

A witch bottle is a counter-magical device used to ward off witchcraft. The first documented reference to a witch bottle dates from the seventeenth century in England. A witch or folk healer would usually be the one to prepare the witch's bottle. Historically, the witch's bottle held urine, hair or nail clippings. Later in history, rosemary, needles and pins, and red wine were added to witch bottles. According to tradition, the bottle is then buried in the farthest area of the property, beneath the house fireplace, or placed in an unnoticeable spot in the house. The bottle is said to capture evil once it is buried where the ingredients hold it down.

In some cases, seawater or dirt are substituted. Sand, stones, knotted threads, feathers, shells, plants, flowers, salt, vinegar, oil, money, or ashes may be found in other sorts of witch bottles. The 'lemon and pins' charm is a similar magical item. The witch bottle was thought to be active as long as it was kept hidden and undamaged. People went to great lengths to conceal their witch bottles; those buried behind fireplaces were discovered only after the rest of the building had been demolished or vanished.

The witch bottle sounds protective, doesn't it? So why mention it here among the other baneful objects. Because it is closely related to our next object, the vinegar jar.

VINEGAR JAR

Depending on your region of the country, some may call this a 'Souring Jar.' The way it is prepared and even the ingredients used are similar to the witch bottle in that it includes needles and pins. In the witch bottle, they are meant to stab the evil entity or witch that is hounding you. In the vinegar jar, they are for stinging and pricking your target to torment them. The main point of a vinegar jar is to sour the life of your target, to make everything go wrong no matter what they try. You might include sliced lemons, black pepper, red pepper, graveyard dirt, hornet's nest, broken glass, pins and needles, petition papers, photographs, or personal concerns. The jar is then filled with vinegar and sealed. Some choose to burn candles on top of the jar, just as people do with honey jars. Shaking the jar regularly is said to make things worse for your target.

WAR WATER

In Hoodoo, war water is traditionally thrown in an enemy's yard, driveway, or doorstep. Since it is usually stored in a glass bottle, smashing the bottle on an enemy's porch is considered a declaration of war – especially effective if it breaks and, as a plus, they can still read the label. Most people leave the label on the bottle so that their target knows what it is and gets the message. War Water is a mixture of iron rust and other substances, such as graveyard dirt and Spanish moss, and suspended in water or vinegar. As the iron oxidizes and the Spanish moss degrades, it takes on a terrible smell similar to raw sewage, on the verge of being a little worse. Yuck. It can also be used to dress candles and objects in baneful spells.

D.U.M.E.

D.U.M.E. products such as oils, powders, and candles are used for extreme baneful magic against an enemy as it stands for 'Death Unto My Enemies.' Not being a worker that would ever partake in death spells, I prefer to work with this oil and candle with the intention of 'destruction unto my enemy.' Since your intention plays a large part in the spells you cast, seriously think about why you want to perform this kind of work.

GOOFER DUST

In practice, it was frequently used to inflict disease on victims, such as limb swelling or blindness. It's made in various ways, but the most common ingredients are graveyard dirt and snakeskin. Ash, powdered sulfur, salt, powdered bones, powdered insects, dried manure, herbs, spices, and 'anvil dust' (fine black iron debris found around a blacksmith's anvil) are all possible additions. The Bantu kufua and the Ki-

Kongo kufa are the origins of the word goofer. Both words mean "to die."

According to excerpts from folklorist Harry Middleton Hyatt's significant research, Hoodoo-Conjuration-Witchcraft-Rootwork, some goofer dust was manufactured from deadly ingredients. In contrast, others were formed from ground-up bones and dirt. "Goofer dust is snake haid, scorpion haid, lizard haid, snake haid dust, scorpion dust, and lizard dust," an interview subject from Fayetteville, North Carolina, informed Hyatt. "That's what you refer to as 'goofer dust.' You get those things, you kill them, you cut out their haids (heads), and you dry that. After you've dried it, powder it up. That's what they refer to as 'goofer dust.'" Place goofer dust in the route of the intended victim to administer it. It can also be strewn on the victim's pillow, in their home, on their clothing, or in the path of where they will walk.

DOLLS

Imitation magic includes voodoo dolls, poppets, and effigies. A piece of hair or a personal item from the targeted individual, for example, will form a mystical relationship between them and their doll. Whatever happens to the doll, it is said, will likewise happen to that individual. It is the notion that comparable actions can produce similar outcomes. The rain dance is a type of imitative magic in which the dancer imitates the falling rain motions. It often works because the dancers continue dancing until it finally rains. The first examples of figurines manufactured deliberately to curse or bind another person date to Assyrian rites from the first millennium BCE. This tradition was also followed in Greco-Roman Egypt in the first and second centuries CE. It was the Egyptian custom to fashion a figurine and then cast a binding curse upon it, often by piercing it with thorns.

What about the term voodoo doll? The term Voodoo implies that the practice has links to either the religion of Haitian Vodou or Louisiana Voodoo; it does not have a prominent place in either. Instead, the term was made popular by the movie industry. The 'voodoo doll,' as we recognize them today, is based on the poppet found in British witchcraft. Each culture that adopted it gave it their own style and variations on the ways to use it. In Hoodoo, they are known as doll babies.

PERSONAL CONCERNS

Personal concerns are elements that have been a part of or worn on the body - a direct link to the target of your spell. Blood, body fluids, hair, fingernails, and worn clothing are possibilities. To gain these personal artifacts, you must be close enough to the person to obtain them. Personal concerns are more common in Hoodoo than witchcraft, although hair is often used in witchcraft spells. Personal concerns could be viewed as a type of contagious magic. The law of contagion is a magical law that states that once two persons or items come into contact, a magical link exists between them until the non-material bond is broken by a formal cleaning, consecration, exorcism, or other act of banishment.

DOUBLE-CROSS PRODUCTS

It is all about trickery. Double-Cross products are created to fool a target into thinking they are being helped. Add a bit of Double-Cross oil into a Love Attracting bath salt to make sure they never find love. Anoint a Money Drawing candle to keep them broke. Pour out half of the Success oil and replace it with Double-Cross so that they never reach their goal. Taking off the Double-Cross label and replacing it with something positive they will use is incredibly sneaky. The possibilities are endless.

GRAVEYARD WORK

Most people have a pretty straightforward idea about what they think graveyard work is, but it has many layers and nuances to its magic. For starters, there is a distinct difference between collecting grave dirt and graveyard dirt. Grave dirt is collected from the grave plot of a specific person to call upon their skills, their knowledge, their notoriety, and sometimes their love for you to help bring about magical change. Graveyard dirt is collected from the property where you find a graveyard, not just one grave. Gather dirt from the North of the graveyard for binding and crossing work or for spells that help you hide something from another. The South of the graveyard is for love or power. The East is for healing or attraction. The West is to bring about an ending or to send something away from you. This is similar to how, after you complete a spiritual cleansing bath, you are supposed to throw some of your bath water in the direction of the West.

But, we are getting ahead of ourselves. There is first something you must do when you approach the graveyard. Traditionally, you must pay a toll to enter the graveyard to do magical work. At the entrance of the graveyard, ask for the permission of the spirits to enter. Wait for an answer. If you are permitted entry, leave nine pennies to the left of the gate. The number 9 is considered a spiritual number for three main reasons:

1. It is three 3's. The ancient Greeks considered 3 to be the perfect number because it represented timing and cycles - birth, life, and death; beginning, middle, and end; and past, present, and future.
2. A powerful number in numerology
3. It mimics the human gestation cycle of nine months, signifying the ending of one cycle and the beginning of another.

It is generally agreed that collected grave dirt should be paid for. Silver dimes are usually payment, but flowers, liquor, and tobacco are sometimes used, and lighting candles at the grave. There are a few simple tools you will need to take with you in order not to look suspicious: a small shovel or spoon, a paper or plastic bag, and silver dimes. Take the spoon and pry back the sod, take the dirt from underneath the sod, drop your dimes in the hole, then cover back up with the sod. Take only what you need. The Bakongo people of Central Africa believed that the earth from a burial contained the spirit of the person buried there. If one knows how to activate and harness the spirit's energy, it is a potent ingredient in magic.

The position on the grave where you take the dirt also matters. Use dirt from the head of the grave for positive work, from the middle (where the heart would be) for love work, and dirt from the foot of the grave is reserved for negative or baneful work.

In the movie, Midnight in the Garden of Good and Evil (based on John Berendt's book), we see the root doctor, Minerva, in the graveyard preparing to commune with the dead. She explains that the half-hour before midnight is for good work, and the half-hour after midnight is for evil, proclaiming, "we're gonna need a little bit of both tonight." This is actually based on the hands of the clock. When both hands of the clock are rising, it is the right time to perform positive or good work or attract something to you. When both hands are falling, it is the time to get something away from you or for baneful work. It is said you should not perform magic when the hands of the clock are on opposite sides.

Because various spirits have different energies, it's important to pick the right grave. The option you choose is determined by the type of spell you intend to perform. Dirt from a baby's grave is recommended for a spell to bring something extraordinary into your life, such as a job or love. Get soil from the grave of someone who loved you deeply (many choose a grandmother) if you're casting a spell to make someone fall in love with you or return to you. If you live far away from where family members are buried, go to the graveyard and explain what kind of work you want to do. Ask if there are spirits present that are willing to help you. You will be intuitively led to the grave that wants to work with you.

Find the tomb of a murderer if you wish to curse someone with an illness, misfortune, or other dark spells. Obtain soil from the grave of a scam artist, a liar, or other troublemakers if you wish family members to argue. The basic idea is that the worse a person behaves when alive, the more trouble their spirit can inflict upon your target.

So, what do you do with the dirt you've collected from a grave or the graveyard? Depending on the type of spell you are casting, it is as simple as using it as you would any other ingredient. Instead of reaching for the favorite herb, grab a pinch of graveyard dirt to anoint a baneful candle, include in a vinegar jar, fix a spell bottle, stuff it inside a poppet, or make your own goofer dust. You can even mix it with the dirt from specific places for spells that are meant to change what is going on in that location.

CANDLE MAGIC

Perhaps it is because I've been making candles for over 20 years, but candle magic is my favorite form of working a spell - or, at least, I always love to include a candle within a spell. The element of fire, which represents transformation, is at the heart of candle magic. Whether turning a petition paper into ashes or keeping a room warm during the winter, fire alters everything it comes into contact with. In candle magic, you're channeling this transformational energy, which encourages and accelerates changes in your life.

Fire is considered the strongest of the elements and the most powerful, magically. Fire is inventive and mischievous. Our ancestors used it throughout all of history to keep away intruders and wild animals. Ceremonially, it was used to cast out illness and disease. It warmed their homes in a natural hearth and home way and helped cook their food. But it could also be used against enemies in sieges to burn wooden fortresses or set fire to entire villages - even as a naval weapon to break an enemy's formation with 'fire ships.' Fire is mutable -- earth and air can either fuel or extinguish it. The interplay with fire depends entirely on the level each element is deployed. Fire is the element of transformation, represented by the Sun and its light.

CANDLE COLORS

The act of burning candles is said to connect the physical and spiritual realms, but different candle colors are also important. When we light a candle of that color, we seek to access the various forms of energy stored in that color.

White – Purity, blessing a relationship or marriage
Pink – For the deep, emotional aspects of love
Red – to signify the passionate side of love
Orange – road opening, bring in new opportunities
Yellow – for happiness in the home
Green – for financial problems that strain a relationship
Blue – healing physically and emotionally
Purple – success in whatever your spell commands
Black – absorb negativity that is damaging a relationship

Sunday – Yellow
Monday – White
Tuesday – Red
Wednesday – Purple
Thursday – Blue
Friday – Green
Saturday – Black

TYPES OF CANDLES

Figural - shaped like people or objects. The solitary man or woman candle is used in magic to represent someone you target with your magic. Hugging couple candles might help to enhance a relationship. Then there are the conjoined candles with a man and a woman: front-to-front (facing each other) brings two people together, while back-to-back is for separating two individuals. There are candles in the shapes of the penis and the vulva for sexual magic.

7-day – these candles are glass-encased candles that are meant to be burnt for seven days. Under the candle, prayers or petitions are placed.

Chime - little tapers that may be found in almost every new age store. Spell candles are the most common name for them, but they're also known as chime candles since they make spinning movements with metal chimes. It takes around two hours for it to burn.

Back-to-back figural candle for breakup work

Offertory - slightly larger than chime candles, so expect a longer burn time. The candle has more surface area for you to carve your intentions onto the surface, making it ideal for spells and rituals that take longer to complete. Because they are the same size as the candle used for power outages, they are sometimes referred to as household candles.

Pillar – pillars are usually thick, free-standing candles with lots of surface for carving words, names, and sigils. They come in a variety of heights and widths.

Drop-in - specifically designed for carving and then dropped into a glass vessel to burn, these candles are for spells that you want to last for about ten days.

Votive - A votive candle, also known as a prayer candle, is a votive offering used in Christian prayer, particularly among the Anglican, Lutheran, and Roman Catholic faiths. It can be used for a quick prayer or spell. It burns for around ten hours and requires a glass votive holder to keep it safe.

Tealights - small candles that burn for three to five hours and are usually housed in a thin metal cup.

DRESSING A CANDLE
When you dress or charge a candle, you're infusing it with the magical energy of plants, minerals, and ingredients that contain mystical properties. For example, there are many 7-day candles on the market with screen printing on the glass with names like 'Come to Me,' 'Reversing,' 'Unhexing,' and 'Money Drawing,' - but they contain no magical elements other than the possible correct color association. Why add these extra herbs, roots, minerals, and flowers? Because they share their lifeforce with your objective. For example, roses are usually gifted on Valentine's Day to symbolize love. We are all familiar with this symbol. If you gave your sweetheart a bag of corn, they would not consider this a romantic gesture! Roses hold love inside them. Daisies evoke happiness. Catnip attracts cats. Thorns are, obviously,

for negative work. And so it goes with the rest of the plant realm.

We put the magic (and ourselves) in direct harmony with the wisdom and innate knowledge of the plant kingdom when we tap into the energies of the Earth when crafting a spell. Some could argue that we align ourselves with the Universe and everything it has created.

Candles put straight into glass or containers can be sanctified and dressed by carving names or letters onto the tops and anointing them with oils and herbs. Use caution. If there is too much oil on the wick, the candle will not burn. Too many herbs will catch fire and interfere with the candle's burning process. I usually rub the top of the candle with my index finger after touching it to an open bottle of anointing oil. It only takes a little. It is tradition to write out your prayer (petition) and place it beneath a 7-day candle.

Figural candles, chimes, pillars, and other non-encased candles can all be carved. The carving does not have to be very detailed. It's enough to scratch names, birthdates, zodiac signs, sigils, and prayers to reveal your intentions. When anointing freestanding candles, rub the oils upward (from bottom to top) to attract things to you and from top to bottom to repel energy. Rubbing powdered herbs and spices into the candle really shows off the carvings you've made.

With so many options, does the size of the candle matter? I would say it does to some degree. It all depends on the spell and how many obstacles are in your way to get the results you want. If it is a small matter of a bit of good luck for the day, a chime candle would be fine. But if you've got roadblocks thrown up on all sides of you, I would choose a larger candle that burns longer. I have always considered the length of time a candle burns to be the number of times your prayers are repeated and sent out into the Universe. According to religious traditions, incense smoke is said to carry your prayers to heaven. With that in mind, do I want my words to go out into the world for two hours or seven days straight? Your unique situation will determine the answer.

SKULL CANDLES
Skull candles are all about influencing the thoughts and actions of others. The intention isn't necessarily harmful, but more of commanding, compelling, getting into the mind of another. Some ways they can be used are:
- Influence a boss about raise or promotion
- Keep another from gossiping about you
- Coerce another to come around to your point of view
- Create confusion for someone who is working against you
- To think of no one else but you
- Get on the same page as you as to where your relationship is going
- Influence a judge before a court date
- Finalize a business deal on your terms

I like to insert quilt pins into the skull candle, with each one representing a different thought. Some people go a step further and dip the pins into condition oils before piercing the skull. For example, if you are trying to get an ex to think about you more and how much they want to come back, dip the pins in 'Return to Me' oil. Another is to rub Boss Control oil on the pins to influence an employer. It has been a long tradition in skull candle magic to 'load' the candle. Loading the candle means to carve out a cavern in the bottle of the candle where you can insert pictures, petitions, herbs, and personal concerns. After loading with your ingredients, melt the wax you dug out and fill in the hole to hold everything in place. You can also take a knife or pen to carve words, names, and thoughts over the surface of the candle. Skull candles can be treated just like any other spell candle where they are anointed with oils and rolled in herbs. I like to use powdered herbs or spices on skull candles.

A WORD OF CAUTION

Before we dive into the spells section, I wanted to offer a bit of advice about hexing and cursing - wait one week before you perform the spell. In the heat of anger, it isn't uncommon to cast a dark spell and then regret it afterward. Clients have come to me asking how to undo a spell because they were too emotional when they worked the magic and didn't think things through. My response? "How do you send water back upstream after you've blown up the dam?" We have all said things we regret in the heat of the moment which could have been avoided if we had simply paused and thought about what we should say next and the repercussions they might cause.

Besides, there is some truth behind the old saying, "Revenge is a dish best served cold." Your target may not realize that you are behind their problems if you wait a bit of time to get your pound of flesh. Also, it gives you time to step back and examine the situation objectively. In the moment, you may have been ready to go immediately to your altar and cast an agonizing death curse on your target! A week later, after you've processed all that happened, you might decide a simple jinx to cause some temporary bad luck is more justified. Or you may just walk away because it is no longer worth your time and energy. On the flip side, if all that anger is still there a week later, you might just come up with an even better hex! When working dark magic against another, the main thing I suggest is to assess, process, and plan.

BANEFUL HERBS & NOTIONS

You will find that many plants that are considered baneful might have an uplifting, positive connotation to them, as well. So, don't be surprised if this list contains some of your favorite ingredients used in good magic. The ingredients listed below are just a small sampling of the many herbs, roots, and flowers you can use in your cursing work. Research each one thoroughly before ingesting or burning, as some may be considered toxic.

ASAFOETIDA - often known as Devil's Incense, is used to compel someone to leave you alone and as an ingredient in many hexing formulas.

BARBERRY ROOT – lay barberry across the path of an enemy to undo or lessen their effect on you. Used to free yourself from the power another holds over you. Used in protection amulets for the home and for children and is also known as Holy Thorn.

CALAMUS ROOT – In Hoodoo, calamus is used for controlling another person or a situation and is often employed in spells of domination. To bend the will of another. In the tradition of witchcraft, it is used in spells for healing and to increase the power of a spell. Do not ingest.

DOG GRASS ROOT - also known as 'couch grass,' is often used in binding rituals, mainly dealing with love. While it is sometimes used for attraction, it is also a useful ingredient in breakup work, especially moving candle spells to separate two people. It can be used as a doll-baby ingredient for controlling a lover.

HONEYSUCKLE - traditionally represents 'loving bonds' and is useful for dealing with infidelity issues. It's a twining vine with fragrant flowers that are used to entangle and bind a lover to you.

KNOTWEED - the very name is a hint - can be used to tie people or situations down. To get rid of an enemy, pack knotweed inside a black cloth or cloth doll along with the person's name, sew it up, and bury it.

LICORICE ROOT - sometimes used as an ingredient in binding spells. Used in spells intended to influence another person and compel them to obey your commands.

MORNING GLORY - many don't know that High John the Conqueror root is related to the morning glory. Also known as bindweed, it binds and stifles another person's will.

MULLEIN – sometimes ground and used in place of graveyard dirt and often used in dark magic spells and to raise spirits. On the flip side of the coin, mullein is hung over doorways as a powerful barrier against demons and evil spirits. Protection against nightmares. Also known as Candlewick plant, Velvet back, and Feltwort.

MUSTARD SEEDS - leave on someone's doorstep to sew strife and discord. It is said that if this seed is strewn around the trunk of a fruit tree on the first evening of a full moon, that tree will not bear fruit. Black mustard seeds (sometimes called brown) are particularly favorable in baneful work. Used to confuse your enemies.

POPPY SEEDS - used in various types of baneful magic, poppy seeds have sometimes been used in death ritual magic. In Hoodoo, they are used for confusion and disturbance, mainly in legal matters, and for creating mistakes in court paperwork. Used for causing couples to argue. Associated with eternal sleep and death rituals.

RED PEPPER FLAKES – Most often used in enemy work, it is an ingredient used in 'Hot Foot' work, and some sprinkle it directly in the path of where their nemesis would walk. A traditional ingredient in souring jars as well. Magically, it is used to create an uncomfortable heat.

SLIPPERY ELM - when buried near their home, it is used to divide a married couple.

SNAKES SHEDS - the shedded skin of a snake is used in hexing and crossing work to cause bad luck, misfortune, or to get someone to leave. It is one ingredient often used in making Goofer dust.

SULFUR - also known as brimstone. Sulfur can be used to assist in the removal of magic. It can be used to prevent or remove undesired spells, as well as to counter opposing magic and, if necessary, to rid oneself of unwelcome spirits and creatures. Warning - burning sulfur can release toxins and is sometimes explosive.

VANDAL ROOT (VALERIAN) - is sometimes used to replace graveyard dirt. Also used for darker magic to summon demons and spirits and as an ingredient in baneful spells. Valerian is supposed to aid in the discovery of hidden information while seeking the truth behind secrets. The pungent odor is often compared to the smell of dirty socks.

WORMWOOD - when burned with sandalwood as an incense, it aids in conjuring and conversing with the dead. Use in binding, exorcism, and protection spells.

Morning Glory

BANEFUL HEXES & CURSES

BINDING SPELLS

This is to cancel out someone's power over you (or others) so that their influence dwindles to nothing. The ingredients are simple: something to represent the person you want to bind, a box of toothpicks, a small cloth bag, and twine. You can use your target's picture, a doll to represent them, or even a copy of their signature if you have it. First, drop about ten toothpicks in the bottom of the bag. Snap in half if you need to so that they will fit in the bag. Place the object that represents your target into the cloth bag. If you have or can get a binding anointing oil, rub some on the inside of the bag. Throughout the entire process, imagine binding your target's power so that it can no longer escape into the world. Now take another ten toothpicks and drop them into the bag on top of your target. Seal the bag. Unwind at least a yard of twine but don't cut off the spool and set it aside. Grab a handful of toothpicks, hold them against the bag, and grab your twine. Wrap tightly around the bag a few times, flip the bag over and lay more toothpicks on top of it. Wrap again. What you are trying to do is to make a cage of sticks around the bag. You can use many methods to achieve this, so feel free to experiment - there is no wrong way. When you have a reasonably substantial cage of toothpicks around your bag, begin binding with the twine until it is completely covered and no toothpicks can work their way loose. Tie to the tallest branch of a tree that you can reach. Bonus - if you can plan this spell ahead of time, drizzle binding anointing oil over the toothpicks, then set them out to dry on paper towels for a few days before using.

MIRROR BINDING SPELL

To boost this spell, perform on a Tuesday, which is thought to be the best day for binding and protection spells. What you will need:

- Mirrors
- Yarn (preferably black)
- Paper & pen
- Picture or name paper of the person you are binding
- Candle (black is best)
- Matches
- Salt

On the paper, write the name of the person you want to bind or use their photograph. Place the paper or photo between the two mirrors, with the mirrors facing each other. Wrap the yarn around the mirrors several times, tying a knot each time. Repeat your intention as you make the knot, such as "I bind you from harming me." Continue wrapping the yarn until you have repeated the process at least fifteen times. Resume talking while you wrap. "You won't have any negative impact on my life anymore. You will reap the consequences of your actions." It doesn't have to be exactly like this; all that matters is that it resonates with you.

Dig a hole. Continue to reiterate your intention. Place the mirrors into the hole with the final knot facing up, then spit on it. Light the candle and pour the wax onto the mirrors/yarn, concentrating on your intention and sealing the negativity inside. Bury the candle with the mirrors when it dies out. Pour a circle of salt around the hole once it's covered to keep the spell intact. Walk away.

SIMPLE FREEZER BINDING

This is a very straightforward piece of magic. Write out the name of your target on a piece of paper. Now turn the paper clockwise and write out your petition stating what you want to happen and what they will no longer have power over. Fold the paper away from you and place it in a ziplock bag. Pour some muddy water into the bag, seal it, and put it in the freezer. Keep there for as long as you want the binding to last.

A WITCHES BINDING SPELL

This is a good example of old Appalachian spells from a time when they felt the need to protect themselves against witchery. This spell is intended to prevent a witch from bewitching a child. It is called 'binding' in local tradition's vernacular, slightly different from other 'binding' spells. Take nine stalks of red thread that have been braided together and tie nine knots in them while saying, "As I knot this string, so I knot you three times three. I bewitch you, witch, and none can do so more." Place the knotted string in a tree for nine days or until it rots away completely.

These folk magic herbal charms often employ natural objects such as roots, herbs, stones, bottles, animal skulls, etc., to provide physical evidence of their magical power. Another example can be in this charm for protection against witches (who, at the time, were thought to be human-like creatures that possess the ability to assume animal forms at will.)

BANISHING SPELLS

COCONUT YOUR LOUSY NEIGHBOR

When you want to get a neighbor to move away, first buy a coconut and cut a hole in it. Drain the coconut water. Let it sit out with the hole facing downwards for at least two days to allow it to continue to dry out. Get a cork and trim it down to fit inside the hole. You will need dirt or gravel from your neighbor's yard from an area you know they have walked over, preferably near their door. If you need an excuse to go onto their property safely, pretend you have been expecting an important piece of mail and ask if they received it by mistake. Gather your foot track dirt or gravel before knocking on the door in case they linger in the doorway. Put their foot tracks inside the coconut along with red pepper flakes. Take the coconut to a river, stand with your back to the water, and throw the coconut over your left shoulder into the river. Walk away.

THE STUPIFYING GO AWAY FOREVER SPELL

What you will need:

- Black candle
- Incense
- Powdered red pepper
- Target's photograph
- Envelope and stamp
- Pen
- Hot foot oil
- Pin or needle

Light the candle and incense. Mark the candle with your target's name, dress it with Hot Foot Oil, and sprinkle it with Red Pepper. Prick the target's photo with the pin nine times (to pierce their thoughts), encouraging them to go away. Five Spot the photo with Hot Foot Oil, then sprinkle it with red pepper.

Seal the photo in an envelope on which you have written their name care of General Delivery to someplace far, far away. Do not include a return address on the envelope. Smoke the envelope in the incense and make your prayer or petition by calling their name, followed by Matthew 5:13, which states: "You are the salt of the earth; but if the salt loses its flavor, how shall it be seasoned? It is then good for nothing but to be thrown out and trampled underfoot by men." Place the envelope under the candle (face down). When the candle burns out, drop the envelope in the outgoing mail.

- Carolina Dean

MOVE AWAY WILLOW TREE SPELL

This is based on an old Hoodoo spell to get a neighboring enemy to move away.

Take the branch of a willow tree from its North or South side – you do not want a branch that the sun shines on in the morning or evening. Take the branch home and strip it clean until it is smooth. It should now resemble a whip. Rub the branch down with a small amount of oil (olive, canola, peanut, etc.), then sprinkle the branch with black pepper. Every day for three weeks, take to your enemy's house and whip against the ground on the edge of their property. (Their porch steps are better but doing this for three weeks straight seems a little risky.) If you cannot approach their home, print out or draw a picture of their house and include the house number. Swat that drawing with the branch every day for three weeks.

At the end of the 3-week period,

- burn the paper and collect the ashes.
- Take the ashes and the branch to a graveyard.
- Dig a hole in the center of a grave,
- drop in the ashes, plant the branch in the hole.
- Turn and walk away without looking back.

DOWN THE RIVER BOTTLE SPELL

Bottle spells thrown into running water usually send a person away from you – to a different location. If you live near a river, even better.

What you will need:

- small bottle – between 2 and 4 ounces
- nails
- lemon juice
- Cast Out and Banish oil or some typing of Banishing oil
- picture of your target
- red pepper
- access to a river or some other running water

If you do not have a picture of your enemy, write their name on a piece of paper and then write your petition over their name. If you do have a picture, write your petition over it stating exactly what you want to happen. Fold it away from you as many times as possible and place in the bottle. Drop into the bottle the nails, peppers, and about 1/3 of the bottle of Cast Out and Banish oil. Fill to the top with lemon juice, cap, and shake while re-stating your intention. Take to a place of running water, such as a river, and restate your intention again. Throw as hard as you can into the water and walk away without looking back.

HOT FOOT POWDER RECIPE

1 teaspoon cayenne pepper
1 teaspoon black pepper
2 teaspoons graveyard dirt
1 teaspoon sulfur powder
2 teaspoons salt

You want the graveyard dirt to be completely dry before adding it to the mixture. Crumble as much as you can with your hands and lay out to dry on a baking sheet for a few days. When it is completely dry, you can turn it into powder by using a coffee grinder or your mortar and pestle. You may want to wear a mask before dealing with this much pepper. Add the rest of the ingredients and mix thoroughly. Sprinkle where your target will walk through it. If it still seems like it would be too visible, mix it with some regular dirt to help disguise it.

Hot foot is primarily used in Hoodoo. In witchcraft, you may find similar powders called 'banishing powder.' Some of the ingredients found in the witch's version of hot foot are:

- Peppers, just like hot foot
- Cinnamon
- Bay laurel leaves
- Dragon's blood
- Sea salt
- Asafetida
- Ginger powder

GET AWAY FROM HERE SPELL
Write your target's name on a piece of paper nine times. Sprinkle with hot foot powder. Fold the paper away from you. Bury in the yard or a pot but be sure to mark the spot somehow so you can find it again. Every day for nine days, go out at sunset and pour a little War Water on the spot. On the morning of the tenth day, dig up the name paper, drive to a railroad tracks, and leave it there.

SPELLS OF REVENGE AND SORROW

DROWNING IN REGRET SPELL

This curse makes the target feel the consequences of their deeds by weighing them down with regret, drowning them in their own bad choices. First, get a large canning jar and set it aside. You will be crafting a doll out of sticks - having the jar ahead of time will help you determine your doll's size. You will need two sticks, one of them forked. Take the forked stick (think of how a slingshot looks) and turn it upside-down. The fork creates the two legs, with the straight end being the body and the head. Take another straight stick and lay across to create the arms and begin wrapping twine around it to keep the sticks together. While you are doing this, speak to the doll you are making and call it by the name of your target. Now take a heavy rock or stone and secure it to the doll's body with your twine. Fill the jar with water and speak into it, stating what you want your target to feel like, for example: "you will be weighted down with regret over how you treated me. Nothing will work for you until you do right by me." Of course, you should decide on the wording based on your situation. Put the stick doll in the jar headfirst. The stone should make it sink. If not, you need a heavier stone. Cap the jar and put it in a dark closet or in a shed outdoors where it won't be found. As long as they remain in the jar, they will be weighed down by the guilt of their bad behavior. Many people choose to burn black candles on top of the jar once a week to keep the energy flowing.

LIVE ANTS INSIDE YOU

As mentioned earlier, this type of curse known as 'live things inside you' falls under the category of magical poisoning. Buy a beef liver from your local grocery or butcher and cut off a piece about the size of your fist. Cut the liver piece open but do not cut through or separate it. Write out the name of your target and slide inside the opening in the liver. Sew shut with black thread. Take the liver to an area with a large anthill and leave the liver beside it. As the ants begin to eat away at it and carry it off in different directions, your target will be cursed with the sensation of live ants crawling inside them.

BLISSFUL ASHES

This spell is to turn someone's happiness into sadness. What you will need:

- Black pepper
- Clove powder
- Dried stinging nettle
- Water from the toilet
- Paper
- Photo or the target or write their name seven times on a piece of paper

On the paper, write the target's name and, if you have a photograph of them, place the photograph on top of the paper. Place one drop of toilet water on each corner of the paper and one in the center. Allow to dry. Fold the paper in half and then fold the ends to form a packet, leaving one side open. Fill the packet with the dry herbs and spices. Fold the packet's mouth closed. Concentrate on the wrongdoings the target has committed against you as you drop them onto the paper. Imagine them having a restless sleep, crying, and standing in a filthy house because they are too depressed to clean. Set a corner of the packet on fire, then drop it into a fire-resistant container. Drive the ashes to a questionable part of town and dump the ashes out the window. Keep driving without looking back.

MAY YOU ALWAYS THIRST

This is a spell to torment your enemy with a dry mouth and constant thirst. What you will need:

- Small jar
- Whiskey
- Rock salt
- Small black candle
- An anointing oil such as Dark Arts or similar
- Coffee grounds

First, fill the jar ¾ of the way full with the rock salt and set it aside. Carve the name of your target into the black candle and anoint it with your Dark Arts oils using a downward motion, from the top of the candle down to its base. Place the candle in the salt, light it, and allow it to burn down. When the candle has finished, add a teaspoon of coffee grounds to the salt, then spit on the coffee grounds. Cover the salt with the whiskey, then seal the jar. Bury in the yard if you want to make the spell more permanent, or, if you want this to be a temporary spell, shake the jar every day until you feel they have learned their lesson. Go to a crossroads and pour out on the ground.

WANDERING RAILROAD SPIKE SPELL

To make someone continuously move and never satisfied with where they are or what they are doing. First, you will need an article of your target's clothing to make this work, preferably not yet laundered. Cut a small piece from the clothing about 2 or 3 inches square. Go to the railroad tracks and find a railroad spike. You will then dig a hole in the middle of the railroad tracks between the crossties. Put the cloth in the hole, then the railroad spike straight down in the hole. If the hole isn't deep enough, drive the spike down further with a hammer until it is below ground level. Fill back in with dirt, then disguise with gravel or whatever else is on the tracks so that the ground doesn't look disturbed. As long as that cloth stays underground, your target will wander aimlessly from place to place.

THE DICK IN THE DIRT SPELL

What you will need:

- Black penis candle
- Damnation oil
- Graveyard dirt
- Snake sheds
- Red ants
- Red pepper flakes
- Coffin nails
- Red chime candle
- Racoon penis bone (coon bone)
- Brimstone

Carve your target's name into the dick candle. I go from the underside to the base to just under the head. Dress the dick with Damnation oil and sprinkle it with red pepper, shreds of snake shed, and red ants. Drive three coffin nails into the head of the dick. I like to put one right next to the wick. That way, that nail heats up and burrows down the length of the candle like a red hot sounding rod.

Put a good-sized mound of graveyard dirt in the middle of your favorite spell tray and prop the dick upright in the dirt. Light the red chime candle and let the wax drip over the head of the dick until it looks like it's ejaculating blood. Get a fist full of brimstone and blow it onto the candle from all sides to finish the dressing.

Now it's time to set your energy. In most cases, I'm a big believer in clearing your energy of all negativities before casting, especially with cursing. But in this case, you really need to let yourself fall to the dark side for a minute. Clear your mind of everything but the negative emotions this mother fucker causes. Let those emotions boil over. Concentrate all of that rage, pain, and whatever else you've got in the pit of your stomach.

Now put a face on that dick. Visualize him. Make it real in your mind. Let out all your frustration. Scream, curse, threaten, accuse, condemn. Every bit of piss and bile you can muster. Let it out on him. All the negative emotions you just cultivated, send it into the dick. Once it's all out and you begin to calm down, take a centering breath and prepare to pass the sentence.

Say the following.

"(Insert name)

You stand before this court accused of (insert specific sin).

How you plea makes no difference. For I alone stand as judge. I alone stand as jury. And by my hand alone does the axe fall.

You are found guilty.

And I sentence you to suffer, damned and condemned. May the pain you've inflicted on others be revisited on you tenfold. May you feel the pain of fire and nails every time you become aroused. And as I sentence it to death, may your dick shrivel and die.

I have spoken. My word is law."

On that last line, just at the moment where a judge would bang the gavel, break the coon bone in half and throw it in the dirt at the base of the dick. At this point, all that's needed is the smallest concentration of willpower to send this curse on its way. Give it that little push as you light the candle.

This next part is extremely important - just walk away. You will want to check on the candle as it burns and even note how it burns and what it may mean. But you need to spiritually turn around and walk away, leaving this asshole in a heap on the floor. Destroyed, in pain, and alone. He's no longer your problem. Equally as important is to take a cleansing bath afterward to rid yourself of any residual negative energy and prevent any unforeseen blowback.

-Jake Sloan

WRECK THE HOMEWRECKER

Get a figural candle that matches the gender of the homewrecker and carve this name into it. Then cut 13 X's all over the body with a sharp knife making the X's deep. Place pins in the head, stomach, genitals, buttocks, feet, and hands of the candle. Rub War Water all over the candle, then roll in graveyard dirt and asafoetida (you might want to wear gloves for this part). Throw it on the front walkway or porch, where they are sure to find it.

BREAKUP CANDLE SPELL FOR TWO PEOPLE

- 1 black or red Back-to-Back candle
- Valerian root (finely crushed)
- Red pepper flakes
- 2 red chime candles
- 2 white chime candles
- 2 black chime candles
- Breakup oil
- Table salt

Breakup using a back-to-back candle, cast a spell to separate or break up two people. The figure of a man and a woman is positioned on the base of a heart, facing away from each other. A candle with the lovers facing each other would be used for love or come to me scenario. Carve the names of the people involved, their birthdates, zodiac signs, sigils, or anything else that would tie them to the candle on each side of the candle.

Both candles should be anointed with Breakup oil and rolled in crushed vandal root (valerian.) When it burns, this candle will create a puddle, so place it on a cookie sheet lined with aluminum foil. Apply the Breakup oil to all of the chime candles and roll them in the valerian root. Place the back-to-back candles in the cookie sheet's center, then move slightly to the front. Place the two red chime candles behind the central candle. One white candle should be placed on each side of the red candles. Place one black candle on each side of the white candles at this point. This represents the progression of their feelings for each other, from passion to blandness to darkness.

Carefully draw a line of red pepper flakes from the front of the cookie sheet back to the chime candles, crossing the central candle at the couple's feet. Place a line of salt around the inside edge of the cookie sheet to prevent any of your work from escaping. Light all of the candles and concentrate on the couple fighting, then not caring, and finally breaking up. Gather the aluminum foil after it has finished burning. Place it on railroad tracks so that the couple is separated.

SEXUALITY CURSES

REVENGE OF THE BANANA

This spell is usually performed when a man has sexually assaulted someone or has threatened to. This is meant to curse his penis with burning pain until it no longer works. Take a banana and peel it back but don't completely remove the peel; leave it attached at the base. Take a knife and make a single long incision in the banana, and gently spread it open. Carve his name into the banana on the inside on both sides of the split. Now fill the gap in the banana with cayenne pepper while thinking about the agony your target will feel. Sprinkle again with whole peppercorns. Close the gap in the banana and bring the peel back up around the banana. Push straight pins into the banana on all sides so that the peel stays in place. Wind red thread or yarn around the banana from top to bottom and tie off. Take a large piece of aluminum foil and wrap the banana. Bake in the oven on an aluminum foil-covered cookie sheet at 300 degrees for about 15 minutes. When cool, bury it in the yard.

POLISH OFF HIS KNOB FOR GOOD

Seven-day knob candles are among the most well-known Hoodoo and magical candles on the market. Some refer to them as wishing candles. One candle can be used for seven wishes, with one knob burned each day for seven days. If these unique candles weren't always available, spiritual workers would take a thick taper candle and section it off in seven segments by inserting straight pins. When the candle burned down to each pin, you knew that day of burning was completed. However, it is more traditional to use them for a single purpose to create a more intense, week-long spell versus seven different intentions. At first glance, one might confuse them for a penis candle, which we will use for here. First, carve his name into the candle. You can do this by spreading the letters of his name across the knobs or by putting his name on the bottom. Pour about a capful of Dark Arts oil in your hand, then begin making masturbation motions the length of the candle. When it starts to heat up from the friction, stop and focus your concentration on each knob, starting with the top. The first knob is an itching sensation. The second is an itch that won't stop. The third day is itching and the beginning of a burning feeling. The fourth day is intense itching and burning that brings on tears. The fifth day is stabbing and burning, making him double over in pain. The sixth day is itching, burning, throbbing, and tears. It all becomes so bad on the seventh day that a trip to the emergency room is in order. Or, depending on your situation, the seventh day can be the easing of the pain once he realizes what he's done to you and wants to make amends.

THE SALTED SNATCH

We can't focus all our attention on the men when there are plenty of wicked women who also deserve a little hexing. Traditionally, most spells placed on genitalia are because someone cheated. This is a spell to sexually dry her up for everyone except her partner. You will need a vulva candle or something that represents the female anatomy, such as a peach, a pomegranate, or a flower such as a red canna, an orchid, or an iris. First, write out your petition. Place her name in the center of the paper and start writing what you desire on top of her name. For example, "you only desire me. No other man can excite you. The thought of sex with other men dries up your desire." Word it however you wish.

Place the petition paper inside whatever object you choose to represent her. For argument's sake, we're going to say you chose a peach for this spell, for which you would make a small incision and place your folded paper inside. Get a large jar and pour about an inch of salt into the bottom. Now, cover the peach in Commanding oil. Begin rolling the peach through salt until completely covered. Shove the peach in the jar and cover with salt to the top. Put the jar under the porch. If that is not possible, bury it under the house, preferably below the bedroom. She will be sexually dry for everyone else but you.

FINANCIAL RUIN

NO MORE MONEY SPELL

This spell is when you want someone's finances to stagnate. It isn't meant to take away their money but to make sure they just can't get ahead, no matter how elaborate their efforts are. Take a printed photograph of your target and repeatedly write the word 'stuck' until the phrase covers their face. If you cannot get a picture of them, write their name seven times on paper, then begin writing 'stuck' across it. Fold the paper away from you over and over until you cannot fold it anymore. Wind the black thread around it three times and tie it off. Drop in the bottom of a small jar. Now, one at a time, drop thirteen pennies into the jar. Fill the jar up with molasses and screw on the lid. You will now drive the jar to a still body of water. You don't want a river or a running creek. Instead, find something like a still pond with algae floating on top. Throw the jar in the water and walk away.

EMPTY WALLET SPELL
The simplicity of this spell is pretty ingenious if you step back and think about what an empty wallet signifies. Go to the store and buy a new wallet in the original packaging. Make sure there is nothing in it, not even stock photographs. Have it gift wrapped. When you get it home, take a piece of poster board and draw a large circle on it. Place the wallet in the center of the ring. Now create a circle of pennies, facing down, around the outside of the drawn circle. Light four black chime candles outside the circle of pennies at the north, south, east, and west. When the candles have finished burning, dispose of the poster board in the trash. Then take the pennies to a store parking lot and drop them where they are sure to be found and picked up. Mail the empty wallet to your target, preferably on their birthday or Christmas, when they would most likely be sure to keep it and use it (because it seems less like a mistake.) Make sure not to include a return address!

LIARS AND GOSSIPS

FREEZE OUT THE GOSSIP
What you will need:

- 7 clove buds
- 2 tablespoons salt
- Aluminum foil
- Paper and pen
- Tongue Tied or Stop Gossip oil

This spell has fundamental ingredients for freezing out the malicious words of a gossiper. Cut your aluminum foil into a five or six-inch square. Write out the offender's name on a piece of paper seven times and fold it away from you three times. Lay on the center of aluminum foil. Drop the seven clove buds on top of your petition, then cover with the salt. Now, pour a healthy dose of your favorite brand of condition oil for gossip. Fold aluminum foil into a tight packet and put it at the back or bottom of your freezer.

MOJO TO SHIELD AGAINST A LIAR
Carrying a black mojo bag containing sea salt and violets could help block lies from being told to you. Violet shields against deception, sea salt is banishing, and black absorbs negativity. Carry with you to keep liars away or protect yourself from becoming the victim of someone else's lies.

LOVE LIFE HEXES

RED ONION SPELL

This is an old Hoodoo spell where the onion symbolizes the tears you want to bring to a couple's home. To break up a relationship, write the pair's names on a little piece of paper, with each name going up the page diagonally in different directions so that their names form an X.

Using a red onion, chop it in half twice to create four equal pieces. Put the onion slices and their name paper in a jar. Pour the vinegar into the jar after it has been warmed up but not heated. Keep it hidden in a dark, out-of-the-way location. You can use the jar to start a fight between the couple by taking it out and shaking it.

9-9-9 SPELL

An old Hoodoo spell to separate two people. You will need nine black candles. 4-inch chime candles would work quite well for this spell. Anoint the black candles in a little olive oil, then roll them in black pepper. Burn one every evening at 9:00 pm for nine minutes for nine days. This could be brought up to date by anointing the candles in Breakup oil before rolling them in the pepper. Since each candle was only burned for nine minutes, there will be leftovers. Bury remains or throw them away. Or, save and repeat the spell one month later if needed. Alternatively, you could take one larger black candle, such as a pillar, and light it every evening at 9:00 pm for nine minutes for nine days.

DRY THEIR LOVE UP

To make the love between two people dry up and wither away. Write each of their names on a separate rose petal. Take a small jar, place one of the rose petals in the bottom, and fill the jar halfway with salt. Drop in the other rose petal. Fill up the rest of the way with sand. Take a piece of alum and push it into the sand. Screw on the cap, then bury it in a graveyard.

EXPEL THE JEZEBEL

This spell is used when a man finds out his wife has been unfaithful, and he wants her to leave the house without argument or drama. Jezebel Root is used to establish female dominance and entice a male lover. Historically, prostitutes used it to lure male clients. Jezebel Root has similar magical properties as Orris Root (Queen Elizabeth Root). Take a good-sized Jezebel root and carve her name into it. Drop into a wine glass and cover with red wine. Cover the glass with aluminum foil and set it in the corner of a dark closet for three days. On the morning of the fourth day, remove the root and set it out to dry. Throw the remaining wine off your property in the direction of the West. When the root has dried, cut it into small pieces. Sprinkle some around where she will walk, such as the driveway or the below the front porch steps. Take a few more pieces and drop them into an envelope, and mail to an unspecified address across the country.

COMMANDING & CONTROLLING SPELLS

YOU WILL DO AS I SAY

To order someone to do something you want. Write your target's name seven times on a small sheet of paper. Do As I Say oil should be applied to the four corners and the center. Fold the paper towards you, then turn and fold it again. Light a purple candle and begin dripping wax onto the paper until both sides are thoroughly sealed. Carve your name on both sides of the wax, then seal it with extra purple wax on both sides. Place in a purple cloth bag, tie off the drawstrings, and hang from the top of a cupboard or pinned above a doorway.

BRING A MURDERER TO JUSTICE

A spell to cause an on-the-run murderer to get caught by the police. You could also use it to reveal the identity of a murderer to the authorities. Take a green bell pepper and carve out the top the same way you would the top of a jack-o-lantern. If you know the name of the person who committed the murder, write their name on a piece of paper and the victim's name on the back of the paper. If no one knows who committed the crime, write 'murderer' in place of a name. Fold the paper towards you and drop it inside the bell pepper. Now clip off a strip of blue fabric and drop it inside the pepper. Blue was the original color of a policeman's uniform. You will need two objects - one from the crime scene and one from the police station. They can be something as simple as a piece of gravel, a pinch of dirt, or a blade of grass. Drop both inside the pepper and put the top back on the pepper. Wind blue thread around the pepper so that it stays shut. Take pepper out to the country and bury it in a field where cattle will roam across it. If that isn't possible, bury them in the woods (where murder victims are often found.)

COMMAND HER!

Recorded in Georgia in the 1940s, this spell is no doubt much older. If a man thinks his woman has a wandering eye and wants to control her to stay home and be only with him, he will need a strand of her hair, a few strands of hair from a horse's tail, a piece of paper, and a needle. The first thing is to take her hair and the horse's hair and begin rolling them between the fingers, twirling together. If she has long hair and you can obtain a strand, braid it when two horsetail hairs. Now take a piece of paper and write both names down - his at the top, hers at the bottom. He then takes the needle, pricks his thumb, and presses a drop of blood over his name. A drop of perfume is placed over her name. Put the hair on the paper so that it touches the blood and fold once towards you. From there, the paper is rolled towards you. Bury only two inches deep in a place where she must step over it often, such as the base of her porch or walkway.

CONTROLLING OIL RECIPE

Controlling products are formulated to get others to follow your direction and commands regarding their thoughts, opinions, and actions. Excellent for skull candle work to reorganize another's thoughts towards your way of thinking. An old Hoodoo trick to use in the workplace to control situations with your boss is to print out your boss' picture, write your controlling petition over it, and anoint it with controlling oil. Fold towards you and place in your shoe. When speaking with your boss about situations that concern you or new ideas, tap your foot.

What you will need:

- Empty bottle
- Calamus root
- Licorice root
- Rosemary leaves

Add a pinch of each ingredient to the bottle and top off with olive oil or another carrier oil of your choice. For three days straight, burn a small purple candle beside the bottle, shaking the bottle right before you light it. On the fourth morning, the oil will be ready to use.

CLEANSE OFF AN ENEMY'S PROTECTION

- 1 White figural candle (male of female)
- 3 yellow chime candles
- 1 teaspoon hyssop herb
- 1 bottle Road Opener oil
- 1 bottle Do As I Say oil
- 1 bundle of white sage

First, carve into the candle your target's name and any personal information you know about them onto the candle. Go down the candle, carving from the head down to the feet. Place the candle in the center of a fire-safe bowl or deep tray, something that will hold water. Add water to the vessel just to the top of the ankles of the figural candle and sprinkle the hyssop into the water. Add a capful of Road Opener oil to the water.

Dip your fingertips into the water and begin to rub downwards on the candle, taking care not to get the wick wet. As you do this repeatedly, pray or speak words such as:
"I cleanse you of all the walls around you.
I wash away your field of protection.
I open up all your defenses.
I wash away your words, power, actions, and magic."

Light the white sage and blow the smoke across the candle nine times, repeating the words you spoke.

Anoint the yellow chime candles with the Do As I Say oil and place them on the outside perimeter of the bowl, forming a triangle. Light the figural candle. Light the yellow chime candles. When all candles have burned, gather up whatever is leftover and bury it on your own property. Your target is now at your mercy.

CONFUSION

MUDDLE THE MOTHER-IN-LAW
This spell could be used on anyone, but the idea of a criticizing mother-in-law who has come to visit would be an excellent choice. It would be considered less of a hex and more of a domination spell. The goal is to scatter the thoughts of a naysayer so that you can take control of the situation and be the one in command. It is as simple as taking a Confusion oil and mixing it with a bit of baking soda. Use this magical powder to clean the guest bathroom (if you have one) while

focusing on your target. You can also dilute it in water and clean all the doorknobs with it. Mix the oil with a little dirt and sprinkle it on the walkway so that it begins its work before your target even enters the house. If you keep the person you are targeting in mind while laying down this trick; it won't affect anyone else in the house. Or, buy a beautiful container of bath salts, add a few drops of confusion oil, and give it as a welcome gift. So, in simple terms, it is a spell of influence meant to break the concentration of your nemesis. If you cannot obtain a Confusion type oil, mix two parts lemongrass oil with one part eucalyptus and a pinch of valerian root. Skip the valerian root (unpleasant smell) if you plan to enchant a bath salt.

SCATTERED THOUGHTS AND BODY PARTS

Confusion work is good to perform right before you plan to do work to undo a spell someone has cast against you. That way, you weaken the hold they placed over you just long enough to sneak in and cancel out their dirty deeds. Of course, the motivation doesn't have to be as dramatic as a curse. You can also confuse a co-worker or anyone else you are competing with. Use for court cases to confuse the opposing lawyer to weaken their case. For this spell, you will need several types of anointing oils or powders such as:

- Confusion
- Love
- Dark Arts
- Happy Home
- Passion
- Better business
- Reversing

Feel free to make your own selections. The objective is to choose several formulas that create conflicting emotions. After collecting your supplies, the first thing to do is to cut out a paper doll that includes the head, legs, and arms. There are templates all over the internet you can copy and print (which can also be used as a "voodoo doll" pattern.) Write the name of your target on the doll along with any other personal information you know about them. Anoint the doll with all the oils, scattering them all over the body. Just go wild, adding dots of each one here and there - everywhere! When you have finished, set it aside and allow it to dry (if you used oils.) Once dry, begin tearing or cutting the doll into tiny pieces of confetti. Divide the confetti in half. Now get in your car and drive around town until you find two conflicting locations to drop your confetti. You want to find two places with completely contradicting energies. Examples might be a concert and a yoga studio, a church and a strip club, a garden center and a junkyard, a health food store and a donut shop, a birthday party and a funeral - you get the picture. The point is to pick two places that evoke utterly different emotions or mindsets. Tip: if you'd rather not spread confetti in a public place, you can always burn the doll and separate the ashes.

SPELLS OF SICKNESS

THE CATFISH CURSE

Write your target's name on a small piece of paper no bigger than your thumb. Fill the paper with their name as many times as you can on both sides. Fold the paper away from you as many times as you can. Take a whole catfish (better if you catch it yourself) and stab a hole into the fish near its tail. Stuff the name paper into the hole in the fish. Release the fish into a body of water. Your target's mental health will gradually begin to eat away.

GIVE THEM AN ULCER

Take a cloth doll and make an incision in the stomach area. Sprinkle inside a healthy dose of cayenne pepper and black pepper. Take nine thorns and drop them inside, then sew back up. Take the legs of the doll and bend them up over the front of the body and wrap them with twine nine times. Set in the corner of a dark closet. An alternate method comes from an old Hoodoo curse that says to use nine pins and stick them in the doll in alternating directions to make X patterns across the stomach. If the person you have placed this curse on turns over a new leaf, and you want to remove the spell, first unbind the legs. Then cut the incision back open and pour cold milk into the 'wound.' Bury it in the yard and sprinkle it with sugar before covering it up with dirt.

CORKING CONSTIPATION SPELL

This spell is meant to cause a condition in the bowels causing constipation. If it continues, it can lead to more serious problems. Take a piece of black construction paper and cut out a two-inch square. You will need fresh chicken manure. Take a toothpick and dip it in the manure to use as 'ink' to write your target's name on the black square. Fold away from you once, then roll up. Drop into a small glass vial (one that has a cork.) It will be tricky to accomplish but take the handle of a spoon or a stick and begin forcing lard or shortening into the vial. If it is too sticky to get much in, you can top it off with liquid cooking oil. Cork the vial and bury it in the backyard at sunset. If you can bury it in your target's backyard or throw it under their back porch, even better.

BAD LUCK

INTO THE PIT

This spell is usually used against a rival that you want to keep down and prevent them from succeeding or getting ahead of you.

What you will need:

- Paper
- Black marker
- Hand shovel
- Pickle juice ¼ cup
- Your own urine
- birthday candle
- Handful of nails

First, take your paper and marker and draw a stick figure representing your target. Write their name in the circle that is the head. Now, begin drawing pointed arrows into the figure on their legs, the arms, the head, and the body while imagining the bad luck they will come up against when they try to do better than you. Dig a hole in the yard (or out in the country) about six inches deep. Burn the drawing of their stick figure in the hole until it is ash. Throw in the nails, the pickle juice, then your own urine. Fill in the hole with dirt and stomp it down with anger, imagining your foot holding down their efforts. Place the candle in the dirt and light it. Sit with it until the candle burns down while you focus on their future bad luck. You can use a birthday candle because it burns down fast enough for you to cast your spell and leave without being disturbed or found out. You can always anoint the candle with a baneful oil for extra power.

HAPPY BIRTHDAY, BITCH!

Is your enemy's birthday coming up? What better time to curse them with bad luck and ruin their day! Receiving parsley as a gift was once considered highly unlucky in England. In the Welsh countryside and other regions of the world, it is thought that picking a leaf or flower growing atop a grave will bring bad luck. So, we're going to use both to make an unlucky dusting powder. First, you will need to visit a graveyard and find a leaf or flower growing out of a grave; even a stem of clover flower or a dandelion would work in this case. Take home and pinch apart the petals if you choose a flower. Do not take flowers that someone left at a grave. It must be growing out of the ground. Allow to dry out completely or, if you are short on time, place it on a baking sheet and put it in the oven on the lowest setting (usually 250 degrees) for about two hours. You can easily get dried parsley from the grocery store. If not, put fresh on the baking sheet alongside your graveyard find. Once all your ingredients are dry, grind into a powder and add a ¼ cup of baking powder. Mix thoroughly. Get a beautiful birthday card and sprinkle the powdered mixture on the inside and outside of the card. Take outside and blow off all the powder. Don't worry, some will remain, but it won't be evident to your target. Mail the card with no signature and no return address. When your target touches the card, the spell will activate. If they keep the card inside their house, bad luck will continue to build.

Detail of an image from a c. 1594 leaflet titled Trier Hexentanzplatz (Witches' Dance Floor), published after the largest witch trials in German history. Note the fireplace mantel with crossed-out markings, which are possibly apotropaic, and the victorious witches at the top of the chimney and flying into the fireplace.

UNHEXING

Uncrossing is the process of removing a curse or hex placed on a person. I have always believed that in order to perform unhexing magic, it is important to have some understanding of how to cast a hex or curse. To me, if you know how to effectively cast a dark spell, you will have greater success in removing one.

RITUAL CLEANSING BATH

Depending on your culture or religion, there may be numerous ways to attack and expel dark energy. But, as most spiritual workers will tell you, cleansing is king. What I have found to be the most effective is a three-step process where you, spiritually speaking, cleanse yourself, cleanse your space, then lock it down with protection. You need that protective element to create a positive 'force field' around you, your home, and your loved ones. I have had many people come to me asking how to remove a curse over the years. When we begin talking about what they have tried so far, probably 80% of them left out the final step - they didn't use protection so that the curse, hex, or jinx could not get back in. So, while they may have effectively cleansed it off at the moment, it was just a mystical bandaid.

If you honestly believe you have been hexed, you will need to summon all your faith, love, and spiritual energy and pour it into the uncrossing ritual. Believe it or not, I have had a few clients who thought performing the three phases of removal seemed like too much work. "Can't you just light a candle for me to take care of it?" Seriously? No. I cannot. If you are too lazy or disinterested to do what it takes (which is actually a pretty straightforward process) to eliminate a curse placed on you, you are part of the problem. This makes me question if they are cursed or simply their own worst enemy - not willing to take the most basic steps to get through each day as a valuable and productive member of society. "This is too hard. You do it for me." Suck it up, buttercup! Now stand over there in that circle of salt and take care of your business! So, what is my point? It is simple - you have to take an uncrossing ritual seriously with commitment, passion, energy, and vigor. If you are not prepared to do that, don't bother.

HYSSOP UNHEXING BATH

Herbal bathing for magical purposes is an ancient practice with roots in both Judeo-Christian and African religious traditions. Psalm 51:7 reads, *"Purify myself with hyssop, and I shall be pure; wash me, and I shall be whiter than snow."* Hyssop is probably the number one unhexing herb; it is often used in spiritual baths to remove curses and hexes or to 'baptize' you as new when seeking a change. Hung in the home to expel negativity, evil influences and to purify. Below are the instructions for performing a hyssop unhexing bath ritual.

- Take about a tablespoon of dry hyssop and place it in about a cup of boiling water, as if you were going to make herbal tea
- Draw a bath and light white candles, placing it on either side of the bathtub — either on its ledge or the floor below.

- Take a bowl into the bathroom with you (more on this later). Pour the herbal bath tea into the water; feel free to strain if you wish.
- Step into the bath and bathe with the intention of removing all negativity from you. The water should only be ankle-deep as you will remain standing to perform this bathing ritual. You may say your favorite prayer while bathing. (This is a spiritual bath — not one where you use shampoo and soap). When you have finished, collect a bowl of your bath water and set it aside.
- Towel dry and blow out the white candles. Take the bowl of bathwater outside and throw it in the direction of the sunset (West), preferably off of your own property.

The first step is spiritual bathing. In the ritual above, I go over the basic steps to perform the bath itself, but let's explore the energy behind it. First of all, don't schedule it on a day you will be rushed or distracted. You want to focus all your energy on the work you are performing. When you put the hyssop in the water to boil, pray into the water while it comes to a boil. You can even take a spoon and write sigils or protective emblems into it. When you light the white candles, do it with focus. Picture in your mind how they are not just plain candles but two flames of energy that help to transform your bathtub into a baptismal font. If you wish, carve prayers or symbols into the candles and anoint them with holy water or oil. You may also add holy or blessed water to the bath as well.

You can chant, pray, or recite a spell during the bath - whatever fits your religious preference. Gather up the water in handfuls and pour it over your head and body. Take your hands and forcibly remove the water back into the tub by firmly rubbing your hands across your arms, legs, and body. Picture the blessed water you are standing in grabbing ahold of the hex and pulling it out of your pores. With each flick of the hands, you are forcing that dark matter into the tub. Instinct will tell you when it is time to stop. When you scoop up the bowl of water before letting the water out of the tub, look into the bowl and know that the curse is no longer on you. When you step out to towel dry, pat your skin gently as if it were new. Know that you have come out of the water uplifted and transformed. When you throw out the water towards the west, hear the screams of the curse fade away to nothing. When you go back into the house, thoroughly clean the bowl with soap and water. Now, scrub the bathtub clean to remove any remnants of the spell that was once in your body. Use holy water or Florida water to clean it, if you can.

Now you are ready for step two - spiritually cleansing the house. I perform the steps in this order for a simple reason. When your unhexing bath happens first, you become a clean vessel in which to cleanse your property. You begin by cleansing the rooms with smoke. Open what windows you can so that the negativity can release and leave. You can choose incense sticks or cones, palo santo, white sage, rosemary, lavender, juniper, or pine - there are many choices of bundled dried herbs. Go with what feels right to you. In Scotland, it is called 'saining' (also performed with water.) The Indigenous people of

America have a ritual known as 'smudging' as a way to connect with their Spirits. I am aware that there is not only misinformation on the internet about what plants are endangered (when some are not) but also about appropriating white sage. I can tell you that I have had many conversations with Indigenous people on the topic of white sage, and most tell me something to the effect of "we are happy to share our medicine when it is used respectfully." However, many would prefer that non-Indigenous people not use the term 'smudging' because it refers to one of their sacred rituals, which is very different from simply cleansing a house with smoke or getting rid of a pesky ghost. But, using smoke for spiritual fumigation isn't unique to North America. We can trace its origins back to prehistoric times, and our ancestors participated in this custom across the entire globe in one way or another.

When you light the sage, hold it at a 45-degree angle and let it burn for about 20 to 30 seconds before blowing out the flame. The end should glow orange. Get a fire-safe vessel like a saucer (many use an abalone shell) to hold underneath it while you travel through the house to protect the floors from ashes and embers. If you have any trouble keeping your herb bundle lit, loosen or cut the twine around it and spread open the dried leaves a little to allow air in. Gently blow on the end of the bundle to create more smoke.

Begin at the back of the house in the room the farthest away from the front door. If you have a two-story house, begin upstairs in the same way. You want to smoke every wall in the room, in the corners, closets, and doorways. Some people even open drawers. Pray or chant while walking. Then move from room to room until you finally step out the front door. Many people continue the process by cleansing the porch and walking around the house. If you have leftover sage, it is perfectly acceptable to butt it out (like a cigar) and save for another time.

It is now time to cleanse by physically cleaning the house, the same way you would give it a good Spring cleaning. There are spiritual floor washes you can buy to clean the floors or just a bottle of Florida water or holy water added to mop water will do. One well-known product is called Chinese Wash that is especially helpful in cleansing floors, doors, and countertops. It is not only for clearing out negativity but is said to leave good luck and abundance in its place. If you have carpets, take a broom and slightly dampen it with a dilution of water and your choice of spiritual wash. When dry, use it to sweep the carpeted floors. You can always vacuum them ahead of time if you wish.

Now, you are clean and the house is clean. What comes next is protection. You want to hold onto all this good, clean energy you've created and lock out the bad so that it can never come back in. Take a reliable protection oil that was made with real herbs (or make your own) and go back through the house leaving a small dot on the corners of all the window frames and door frames. (Holy water works too.) Go outside and do the same to the outside of your front and back doors and make a straight sweep across the threshold. Anoint the four outside corners of the house. Now walk out and drop a few drops at the four corners of your property, the mailbox, and the two edges of the driveway. You have now created a basic forcefield of protection.

Want to take it a step further? Anoint some protective crystals or amulets and place them around the house. Windows are a good place for amulets to hang. Corners are great for stones. I always suggest to clients that they also anoint a piece of jewelry so that they carry the protection with them when they leave the house. If you don't wear jewelry, bless a charm and attach it to your keyring. Anoint an amulet or talisman of some sort to hang from the rearview mirror of your car and anoint your four tires. Altogether, you should now be about as spiritually protected as humanly possible.

If you cannot throw your bath water out at sunset, at least know which direction is West for proper ritual disposal.

AFTER THE RITUAL BATH

After you have completed cleansing yourself, your home, and created a barrier of protection, it is vital to go about your daily routine with the full knowledge that it worked. Start the day with a smile, pull back the curtains, and let the sunshine in; know in your heart that it is a new day filled with possibilities! However, many people have lived with misfortune for so long that they don't know how to function without it. So, they go about their day as they always did - looking for bad omens, expecting efforts to fail, waiting for the other shoe to drop and bring more bad luck. And so, they fulfill their own prophecy.

The hex is gone. The day is new and clean. But they don't trust that it worked. So, they interact with other people in the only way they know how, putting off this negative, downtrodden, woe-is-me energy that only serves to attract more negativity. According to the law of attraction, people who think positively are more likely to achieve their goals, while those who think negatively are more likely to fail. It is founded on the idea that good energy attracts success in all aspects of life, including health, wealth, and relationships. The theory suggests that removing negative elements from your life makes room for positive ones to come in. Whether you believe in the law of attraction or not, there are some truths to be found in it - kindness is usually repaid with kindness; gossip, backstabbing, and toxic behavior will eventually bite you in the ass. My point? The energy you put out into the world shapes the world in which you live. If you are a joyful person with a positive attitude, the more people want to be around you. If you are Debbie-downer who is always in a funk, others will avoid you. 'Please' and 'thank you' will get you further than demands. You already know this unless you were raised in the wild by wolves. The curse is cleansed. Act like it and watch as a new world unfolds for you.

WARDING OFF EVIL

To protect themselves and their loved ones from evil, ancient cultures frequently used the powers of magical or apotropaic symbols and rituals. Apotropaic magic, often known as protective magic, is used to ward off damage or negative influences, such as misfortune or the evil eye. When applied to magic, 'apotropaic' comes from a Greek word that means 'to ward off' or 'to turn away.' It becomes an umbrella term for numerous symbols placed on a house to keep evil out and specific artifacts imbued with magical qualities that protect those who wear or travel with them.

WITCH MARKS

In Europe, apotropaic marks, sometimes known as 'witch marks' or 'anti-witch marks,' are symbols or patterns carved on buildings, walls, beams, and thresholds to ward off witchcraft or bad spirits. In the United Kingdom, they are frequently flower-like patterns of overlapping circles. The daisy wheel, also known as the hexafoil, is one of the most common witch marks found carved on buildings and barns dating back to the 1500s. The emblem is shaped like a six-petaled flower, as the name suggests. The daisy wheel can easily be sketched with a compass and hence has a very geometrical design. Daisy Wheels range in size and intricacy from a single hexafoil to a network of interconnected hexafoils. One theory about this design is that the evil spirit would become trapped between its concentric rings and would be unable to escape. The daisy wheel pattern is found in many Pennsylvania Dutch hex signs. The double V pattern is also widely seen and is said to represent Mother Mary or Virgin of Virgins. Hundreds of protective marks, including the double V, were found in England's oldest cave, known as the Creswell Crags, in the East Midlands of central England.

When puritans crossed the pond to America, they brought their superstitions with them. Many symbols, including conjoined circles, have been found in New England homes from the 17th century. The symbols were placed in locations of the house where evil spirits could enter, such as fireplaces, doors, and windows. Another typical method of protecting the home from evil spirits was to conceal personal objects, particularly shoes, in the walls of the dwelling. It was believed that a personal item, such as an old shoe, had absorbed the 'essence' of the previous wearer. As a result, the witch or demon mistook the essence for their intended victim and became trapped. Iron was also employed on occasion in the form of horseshoes, old knives, or ax heads.

MAGIC MIRRORS

A 'magic mirror' operates on the premise that whatever is reflected in it, including malicious intent, will be returned to the sender. This is especially helpful if you know who is throwing negative energy your way.

There are various ways to make a magic mirror. The first and most basic method is to use a single mirror. To begin, bless the mirror just as you would any other new magical tool. Place the mirror standing up in a basin of black salt. In witchcraft, black salt has long been used for protection and banishing ceremonies.

Black salt, which is also utilized in both witchcraft and Hoodoo, may absorb negative energy from your surroundings and is frequently used in spells and magical workings to create borders, assist with spiritual barriers, and provide protection.

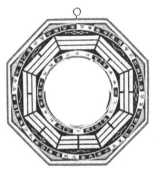

Bagua Mirror

Place anything that depicts your target - the person cursing you - in the bowl, facing the mirror. This might be a photograph, a business card, a miniature toy, an item they possess, or even their name written on a piece of paper. This will return that person's negative energy to them. In Feng Shui, 'Bagua mirrors' deflect or reroute negative energy. They are usually placed outside the house, but if you live in an apartment, you can face it looking out of a window.

HEX SIGNS
Hex signs are a type of Pennsylvania Dutch folk art connected to fraktur (a decorative form of folk art created by the Pennsylvania Dutch and is named after the script associated with it) that may be seen in Pennsylvania Dutch Country's Fancy Dutch culture. Barn paintings began to appear on the landscape in

the early nineteenth century, mainly in the style of 'stars in circles.' On the significance of hex signs, there are two schools of thought. One side regards the signs as talismanic, while the other thinks of them as just aesthetic. For our purposes here, we will discuss their talismanic nature. As much as some would like to argue that hex signs are merely art, there is no denying that the symbols used within them, such as hexagrams, pentagrams, and octagrams, have roots in Germanic paganism.

The Distlefink Hex Sign
An extremely popular Hex sign. Actually a Goldfinch, this bird has the distinction of being called a Distlefink because of its great desire to feed on 'thistle seed' and use the thistle 'down' for its nest.
The bird stands for 'Good luck or good fortune'; the heart for love, and the tulips for faith, hope, and charity.

The German word 'Die Hexe' is thought to derive from Old High German' hagzissa,' meaning 'witch,' and the Middle High German' hecse' with the same meaning. While many of the symbols used are for protection and good fortune, the circular pattern they are painted on was considered to be a witch trap. The word 'hexafoos' refers to a three-toed or triangle mark applied to some Pennsylvania barns to ward off bad spirits and keep them away from the cattle. In recent years, hex signs have become popular as talismans for folk magic among non–Pennsylvania Dutch people. Some neopagans and Germanic heathens have started making hex signs, combining various pre-Christian signs and symbols into the process. Lee R. Gandee, in his book, *Strange Experience, Autobiography of a Hexenmeister*, described hex signs as 'painted prayers.'

PROTECTIVE BURN MARKS

Taper burn markings are deep flame-shaped scorch scars commonly encountered on timber beams in homes constructed in the early modern age (right after the Middle Ages up to around 1800.) They were once assumed to be accidental, but studies reveal that most marks were generated on purpose, as there is evident patterning of the activity. It is believed that the purpose of their construction was to protect the building from lightning - and, more especially, fire. In some ways, it's like immunizing the building - literally 'fighting fire with fire.'

They are frequently found at home openings such as fireplaces, doorways, and windows with distinct tear shapes. Studies of these marks show they were undoubtedly made on purpose due to the consistency of the shape and that many were found in places where candlelight would not have been needed. To create it, a candle or taper was held at a 45-degree angle so that the hottest part of the flame faintly brushed the wood. The technique almost immediately caused sooting on the woodwork, but over time, the burn gradually began to wear into the woodwork. In the Tower of London, over 80 similar marks have been unearthed.

INCANTATION BOWL

Known as a demon bowl, devil trap, or magic bowl, an incantation bowl is an early form of defensive magic that was prevalent in what is now Iraq and Iran at the time of the Middle Ages. This type of bowl was made in Mesopotamia and Syria in late antiquity during the sixth and eighth centuries. It was frequently written in a spiral, starting at the edge and going toward the center. Jewish Babylonian Aramaic is the predominant script used.

An incantation to protect Shrula son of Duktanuba and Qaqay daughter of Kaspasta against evil spirits. Iraq between 6th and 8th century. On display in the British Museum.

They were supposed to serve as devil traps; thus, they were buried face down. They were frequently buried in cemeteries and interred under thresholds, in courtyards, and the corners of recently dead dwellings. Since there are cracks between the walls and the floor in the corners of rooms, these kinds of traps were frequently set there to prevent demons from slipping in.

SATOR SQUARE

This amulet dates all the way back to Roman times and has been discovered everywhere, from the ruins of Pompeii to being found in Scandinavian spellbooks. While the square was once assumed to be a Christian creation, evidence shows that it dates back to a much earlier time and may have Jewish or Mithraic origins (a Roman mystery religion based on the god Mithras). It is written as a square (Arepo under Sator, Tenet under Arepo, Opera under Tenet, and Rotas under Rotas) so that it may be read from left to right and up and down. It is a palindrome, meaning the sentence is the same backward as forward. Create a protective circle around yourself by writing the square on a piece of paper. To activate the paper as an amulet, recite the mantra 'Sator, Arepo, Tenet, Opera, Rotas.' You can also find pendants of SATOR to wear as a necklace. A possible transliteration is: sator, the sower; arepo, with his plow; tenet, holds; opera, with purpose; rotas, the wheels.

SAINT BRIGID'S CROSS

On Saint Brigid's Day in Ireland, it is common to weave a Brigid's cross out of plants called rushes and hang it over doors, windows, and stables to protect the home and buildings from fire, lightning, illness, and evil spirits. On January 31st, the eve of Brigid's feast day, families would gather the rushes together. After feasting, they would weave the crosses and then leave them out to dry in order to receive Brigid's blessings. On the next day, February 1st, the crosses would be hung. Brigid's cross, along with other nationalist symbols such as the shamrock and the Celtic harp, was employed by Irish artists to build a national cultural identity distinct from Great Britain when the Irish Free State attained independence in 1922.

PROTECTIVE AMULETS

Amulets are used for protection to prevent unwanted energies from reaching you like harm, illness, or hexes. I am referring to objects you wear or carry with you to protect you magically, not physically. An excellent example came from the Sheila Paine book, *Amulets: Sacred Charms of Power and Protection*, where she explains that a chunk of meteorite worn to protect against gunfire is an amulet, but a bulletproof vest is not. In 2021, Catherine Yronwode and I teamed up to write the book, *How to Use Amulets, Charms, and Talismans in the Hoodoo and Conjure Tradition: Physical Magic for Protection, Health, Money, Love, and Long Life* which covered over 150 protection charms, amulets, sigils, stones, seals, talismans, and herbs to keep harm away. This is the main reason why you won't see me cover the topic in great depth in this book. Been there, done that. But I did want to include some of my top picks when it came to protection stones and amulets.

TOP FIVE STONES FOR PROTECTION

BLACK TOURMALINE - If you're looking for a powerful stone to wear all the time, look no further than black tourmaline. Known for its ability to transform negative energy, this jet-black stone has a powerful grounding effect. The wearer's negative feelings are banished, turning these dark vibrations into positive ones and often used to create a protective barrier around the house.

HEMATITE - The negativity absorber. The Egyptian pharaohs' tombs were decorated with it. In ancient times, people believed that carrying a piece of Hematite with them on their journey to the afterlife would protect them from evil spirits. When combating negative energy, Hematite acts as a sponge, soaking up negative energy and keeping it from interacting with your aura. Many people wear hematite rings for this purpose, and it is said that when it absorbs all the negativity that it can, the ring will shatter. This is why it should be cleansed often to release those dark energies.

MOONSTONE - For centuries, people have used Moonstone as a personal talisman because of the protection it offers, especially at night. It also has a reassuring, uplifting aspect. It is named after the night sky's celestial ruler. Moonstone is an excellent crystal for calming and soothing its wearer by removing cosmic fog and negativity. It is known as the Traveler's Stone because of its powers of protection.

OBSIDIAN - As lava cools, it forms gorgeous black obsidian. Creating a shield of protection with black obsidian is one of the most common uses of the mineral. Negative energy can be absorbed by carrying or wearing it, and it is also used as a divination or scrying mirror because of its reflective properties. In much the same way, black obsidian is also used to reflect negative energy back to where it came from, making it a good tool in reversing magic.

TIGERS EYE - Since antiquity, many cultures have believed that this stone could protect the wearer from harm. It is a grounding stone that can help clear the root chakra, giving you a greater sense of security in this world. It shields you from negative energy. It was thought to keep the evil eye at bay. Roman troops wore Tiger's-eye as a kind of protection during combat. Its golden color and the fact that it can sometimes resemble a cat's eye give it its name. In addition to yellow, there are also variations in blue and red.

AMULETS

ANKH - The ankh symbol—sometimes referred to as the key of life or the key of the Nile - is representative of eternal life in Ancient Egypt. You often see images of Egyptian Gods and Pharaohs holding the ankh. When used as an amulet, the Ankh is said to give the wearer power and a long, healthy life full of abundance. It was used in burials to carry these qualities over into the afterlife. It is also used in the Coptic Orthodox Church. The ankh is the most widely recognized symbol of African origin in the Western world, and people of African descent sometimes use it as a symbol of African cultural identity.

The Egyptian Ankh

GRIS-GRIS BAG - The gris-gris is thought to have originated with Islamic traditions in Dagomba, Ghana, and has spread throughout West Africa, the Caribbean, and Louisiana's Cajun and Creole populations. Mainly used to protect one from evil spirits, the gris-gris bag was filled with not only protective herbs and curios but also items that made a connection to the person it was being crafted for. The gris-gris bags of today have become more like mojo bags, which can be magically crafted for many different purposes and situations. Mojo bags can also be used as amulets of protection.

HAMSA - The Hamsa Hand, often known as the Hand of Fatima, is a Middle Eastern talisman. It is a protective sign in all religions. It is a talismanic emblem that is thought to protect people from harm and bring them goodness, abundance, fertility, luck, and good health. Some people believe that if the hand is facing with the fingers pointing up, it will protect them while looking down will bring them blessings and prosperity. Khamsah is an Arabic word that means 'five', but also refers to images of 'the five fingers of the hand'. The eye in the center of the hand symbolizes its protective powers against the evil eye. Also known as the Hand of Miriam.

Hamsa hand

IDIOSYNCRATIC AMULETS - You select these charms because they have personal meaning just to you. Since it is unique to your personality, you do not have to follow tradition. Some examples are national flags, flowers, certain animals, birthstones, a family heirloom, or a lock of hair inside a locket. Some may choose a cameo their grandmother owned, or a piece of jewelry given to them when they graduated high school - even a class ring. You can create a ceremony for transforming this personal item into a protective amulet if you wish. Give it a thorough cleansing with smoke, then place it in an ornate dish. Surround the dish with white candles that you have anointed with your favorite protection oil.

PENTACLE - Contrary to popular belief, a pentacle is a powerful protection against evil. Many religions have utilized the five-pointed star symbol, including the Druids and Christians. The Hebrews used the star to represent Truth and the five volumes of Pentateuch, while the Christians thought the points meant the five wounds of Christ. Today it is primarily associated with witchcraft and Wicca. So, what is the difference between a pentagram and a pentacle? The pentagram is the five-pointed star, while a pentacle is a five-pointed star within a circle or on a pendant. The pentacle is usually what is used as an amulet or talisman and may incorporate other symbols and sigils within or around the star. Some people use the words interchangeably.

RELIGIOUS MEDALLIONS - The blessings of particular deities, spiritual entities, or saints are transmitted through religious medallions which can be used as amulets. A Saint Michael medallion is probably the most popular, depicting the warrior angel slaying evil with his sword. A Jesus or Mary medallion are two others that people use to call upon their love and protection along with the popular Saint Christopher 'Protect Us' medallion. Any saint can be chosen according to your preference and what power you need to call on in a particular phase of your life. I wear a chain with a silver cross and four medallions, including one of Marie Laveau. Of course, wearing medals for protection isn't limited to Christianity. You can choose any figure that puts your energy into a safe space.

Saint Michael medallion

SEAL OF SOLOMON - The Seal of Solomon is a signet ring associated with King Solomon in medieval mystical traditions. It evolved in parallel with Islamic and Jewish mysticism and Western occultism. Its design became known as an amulet or talisman, which could be used for protection. It was frequently portrayed as a pentagram or hexagram and provided Solomon with the ability to command demons, jinn, and spirits and communicate with animals. It is the forerunner of the Star of David, which has become the modern-day symbol of the Jewish people. The hexagram, or 'Star of David,' was included on Israel's flag in 1948.

Solomon Seal ring

To alleviate any confusion, The Key of Solomon is a medieval grimoire, or book of magic, wrongly attributed to Solomon. Scholars typically identify the Key of Solomon as a 14th- or 15th-century piece of Latin literature. Most remaining manuscripts date from the 16th to 18th centuries, including translations in several languages, especially Italian. The manuscripts include many sigils, pentacles, and necromantic designs used in invocations and spells. But when people refer to the 'Seal of Solomon,' it refers to that particular symbol on his ring.

TRIQUETRA - The Celtic triangle, often known as the triple knot, was thought to form an impenetrable protective circle. It represents how the physical, mental, and spiritual realms are connected. It is also the symbol of the mother goddess and the moon goddess and was Odin's symbol throughout early Pagan times. It was once on the cover of the Gideon Bible and is often used to represent the Trinity in Christianity. The three equal arcs symbolize equality, the continuous line depicts eternity, and the interweaving symbolizes indivisibility.

Sometimes charms, amulets, and talismans are used interchangeably, but there are important distinctions between them. The term 'lucky charm' refers to a charm intended to bring you good fortune or good luck. These were magic words that might enact a desired outcome, whether sung or uttered. When the crops are doing well, one British spoken charm is to cry, "Bad harvest, bad harvest!" to ward off the jealousy of the gods so they would not destroy the crops. In other words, charms weren't always tangible objects that you carried around or wore - they were spells that you recited to achieve your goals.

The primary purpose of an amulet is to shield the wearer from injury, illness, and hexes. The oldest ancient amulets were made from natural materials, such as roots, nuts, certain beans, and animal bones and teeth. When it comes to amulets, you don't have to do anything to make them magical; they are magical by their very nature. For example, High John the Conquer root is used in Hoodoo as a pocket piece or a mojo hand on its own.

Talismans are usually handcrafted for a single individual. They were traditionally made from a particular metal or gemstone to link them to their wearer. Using teeth, bones, or furs from powerful creatures like bears was considered a way to gain the power of that animal. You can use symbols such as sigils and prayers, but you can also use hieroglyphs, runes, and even Solomon's seals.

SPELLS TO UNCROSS

SPIRITUAL BATHING

DISPEL RUMORS
If someone gossiped about you, this is a modernized version of an old-fashioned southern Hoodoo spell to cleanse away their slander. What you will need:

- Wintergreen oil
- Cinnamon oil
- Van Van oil
- Borax
- Sugar

Take one cup of borax and add to it 2 drops of wintergreen essential oil, 2 drops of cinnamon essential oil, and 10 drops of Van Van oil and knead through the borax until the oils are thoroughly blended in. Now mix in one teaspoon of sugar. Sprinkle about two tablespoons into your bathtub then get in and shower as you normally would, praying away the gossip while you lather and rinse off.

This is not for a soak bath as wintergreen and cinnamon can be too strong on the skin. Your soap suds should mix with the borax mixture and carry the slander about you down the drain. If any is left in the bottom of the tub when you have finished, help it to rinse down the drain and rinse your feet off well. Towel dry as you normally would. Do this two times in one week - once on Tuesday and again on Friday. If you cannot locate borax, use baking soda.

FOOT TRACK MAGIC CLEANSING

This is based on an old Hoodoo rite for removing crossed conditions. It can be used to remove foot track magic (like hot foot) or for cleansing a home of the residue of foot track magic.

What you will need:

- holy water
- ammonia
- powdered horseradish
- Jinx Begone or Saint Cyprian oil
- 3 straws from a broom
- plain water

The implementation is straightforward. Mix roughly a half cup of ammonia with about 5 cups of water in a bucket. a pinch of powdered horseradish, three broom straws, a squirt of holy water, and a capful of Jinx Begone or Saint Cyprian oil. Mix thoroughly. Clean the four corners of the house with a rag or sponge (inside.) If you're worried about the combination ruining your carpets (or anything else), simply wipe off the baseboards in each of your four corners. This refers to the entire house, not just the four corners of a person's room. As a result, you'll have to wander from room to room to touch the structure's four sides. Take it outside and throw the rest on the front porch once you've finished. Pour extra water on the porch to clean it after you've spread it around a bit. When someone enters the front door, the cleansing will now be transported throughout the remainder of your house.

REVERSING SPELLS

PINS LIKE DAGGERS REVERSING SPELL

This spell is to send back a spell that was placed on you. Despite its simple ingredients, it packs a punch when it is thrown back. You will need to have a fire going to complete this spell. First, take a small bottle and fill it full of as many straight pins as it will hold. Fill with water and put on the cap. Just before midnight, begin burning frankincense in front of your fire. At the stroke of midnight, say the name of the person you believe cast the spell on you and throw the bottle into the fire. When it breaks, the spell reverses back to the person who originally cast it.

TORMENT YOUR TORMENTOR

This work is very old and similar spells can be found in Scottish and English folklore as well as Africa and Haiti. You will need a double boiler to melt wax in. You can either buy new wax at the craft store or melt down pillars or taper candles. Keep in mind that most craft store waxes are soft and meant for crafting container candles. You need something firm like a paraffin wax. You will be crafting a wax doll of your target. This could be a person who you believe is doing magical work against you or it might be a bully or even a stalker. You can either sculpt the figure yourself by hand or use a human-shaped candle mold. Just keep in mind that if you intend to sculpt it that you have to let the wax cool enough for you to handle but not so cool that it cannot be shaped. So, this method might require a few rounds of melting and remelting to allow you enough time to create a complete human figure. There are countless sources online to learn the basics of melting wax and candle making.

Before you melt your wax, write out the name of your tormentor seven times on a piece of paper. Or use a photograph of them. Burn and set the ashes aside. Begin to melt your wax. When it reaches the liquid stage, add the ashes you collected along with a pinch of poppy seeds and dried rosemary leaves. Speak the person's name as you stir the wax. Pour in mold (or sculpt) and allow to harden. For seven nights, take the wax doll and pass it through flames over and over. Move quickly, not enough to melt it but enough to torture your target. On the seventh night, throw it into the fire and let it burn and melt. After that, they shouldn't bother you anymore.

PROTECTION SPELLS & RITUALS

THE POWER OF BLOODROOT
Bloodroot is said to bring peace into the home and protect a marriage and can also be used as a replacement for real blood in spells. Toxic if ingested. Bloodroot can be carried for protection against evil and curses. Place in doorways and windowsills to shield the home from evil. If you know of someone who you suspect is working against you, cut the bloodroot into pieces and throw them into their yard.

EGGSHELL POWDER FOR PROTECTION
Save your eggshells in advance to maintain a good supply of protection powder in your home. If you're in a hurry and need some now, break three eggs and rinse the shells completely. Cleaning the shells is

considerably easier if you do it right after you crack them. Allow to dry completely. Place on a baking sheet and dry in the oven on the lowest heat for about five minutes. This is a powerful protective force that can be used in a variety of ways, including spreading it over your property, blowing it across protection candles, sprinkling it under the welcome mat, using it as a mojo bag element, and so on. There are numerous options.

What you will need:

- 3 egg shells
- 1 teaspoon powdered ginger
- 1 teaspoon sage
- 4 tablespoons cornstarch
- Protection oil

To begin, combine the cornstarch and about a half capful of Protect Me oil in a glass bowl. To combine the oil and powder, mix thoroughly with your fingertips, then rub the powder between your hands over the bowl. This rubbing movement will help to distribute the oil evenly throughout the powder. Mix in the powdered ginger and sage until thoroughly combined. You can now begin breaking up your eggshells once they are entirely dry and cool (if you dried them in the oven). The shells can be pulverized into tiny fragments with a mortar and pestle. Some people keep a coffee grinder on hand solely for magical purposes, grinding the shells into powder. When the eggshells are as small as possible, add them to your batch of ingredients and mix again. Because the oil in the mixture may still be liquid, lay the powder out flat and let it dry completely overnight. Place in a bag or a glass jar for later use.

DOORWAY & BOUNDARY CHARM SPELL

This charm spell is used to keep evil away from your house and invite the good inside. Call in blessings and banish negativity.

What you will need:

- ¼ cup sugar
- ¼ cup salt
- 2 small jars
- 1 white chime candle
- 1 black chime candle
- Devil Begone sachet powder
- House Blessing sachet powder
- 2 cross charms
- Blue embroidery thread

Fill one jar with sugar and the other with salt. To the sugar jar, add one Tablespoon of House Blessing Sachet powder. Then, in the jar of salt, add one Tablespoon of Devil Begone sachet powder. Stir each one well until the sachet powders are mixed in thoroughly. Now, place one cross charm in the sugar jar and screw on the lid. Next, put the other cross in the salt jar and screw on the lid. You are now going to burn the white candle on top of the jar of sugar and the black candle on top of the jar of salt.

The next day, open the jars and take out the charm crosses and set them aside. Take the jar of salt to the end of your driveway and begin throwing handfuls into the street. When you have finished, take the jar of sugar, go to the end of the driveway – but this time, turn and face your house and begin throwing handfuls up the driveway while walking towards the house until you return to your doorway. When you have finished, take the embroidery thread and cut a piece off about 6 feet long. Double it over to make it a thicker, 3-foot-long piece. Then tie both of the crosses onto the thread. Nail the thread in the doorway in the space between the front door and the storm door (or where a storm door would normally be.) If this is not possible where you live, hang on a nail or tack just inside your front door. This charm will keep the bad out and invite the good in.

AN APPALACHIAN CHARM AGAINST WITCHES

At midnight on a Saturday take seven hairs from the mane of a black cat and tie them together with three knots, saying "As this hair is knotted so I knot you. As this knot is tied so I bind you." The remainder of the hairs are carried in one's pocket or purse where they are believed to protect against witches coming near the person who carries them.

These hill-folk practitioners also use various colored candles strategically placed around their homes for protection against evil entities that may try to enter through doorways or windows. If there is a window above a doorway in which a person has been sleeping, a green candle should be lit on the other side of the window to protect him or her from harm caused by ghosts and ghouls who may want to enter through that doorway. Another method is to place a black candle within a circle of salt to keep evil entities away from their position for as long as it burns.

FLORIDA WATER PROTECTION BOTTLE
Take a bottle of Florida water and remove the label. Now, cut out a piece of paper about the same size as the original label and write on it the beginning of Psalm 31: *I come to you, Lord, for protection; never let me be defeated. You are a righteous God; save me, I pray! Hear me! Save me now! Be my refuge to protect me; my defense to save me. You are my refuge and defense; guide me and lead me as you have promised. Keep me safe from the trap that has been set for me; shelter me from danger. I place myself in your care.*

Write your name and the names of all who live in your household between the lines of the psalm. Wrap the new label around the bottle facing inward. You can tape it to the bottle with clearing packing tape. Inside the bottle you're going to add:

- Angelica root (to receive blessings)
- Blue cornflowers or lavender buds (for peace in the home)
- Plantain (to prevent theft)
- Pinch epsom salt (to reverse any evil)
- 3 straws from your broom (to keep away unwanted visitors)
- Piece of tourmaline (grounding, but also thwarts complaining neighbors)

Take 3 white chime candles and anoint with Blessing oil. Burn one candle beside the bottle, every day for 3 days. Place a good loaf of bread on the other side of the bottle. Shake the bottle every day.

When finished, use the Florida water to anoint your doorways, welcome mat, front porch, your mailbox. Pinch up the loaf of bread and spread in your yard so that the birds can carry your blessings and protection up into the trees and throughout your neighborhood.

7 CHURCHES SPELL OF PROTECTION
What you will need:

- The dirt from 7 different churches
- Lemongrass herb
- Rosemary herb
- Powdered cinnamon
- 1 black 7-day candle
- Wall of Fire Protection oil
- Bundle white sage (or another bundle)

First, print out psalm 27 and anoint the paper with Wall of Fire Protection oil. Keep in your pocket as you go out and collect a small amount of dirt from 7 different churches.

Use a mortar and pestle, an herb grinder, or a coffee grinder and powder your lemongrass and rosemary herbs. Combine the dirt from the seven churches and add your herbal powder along with powdered cinnamon --- all herbs and spices of protection.

Poke 7 holes into a black 7-day candle and anoint the candle with Wall of Fire or another protection oil and set aside. Place your dirt mixture in a fire safe bowl or dish and place the candle in the center on top of the dirt. (You could also use a 7-day knob candle, burning one knob a day. If you choose this, anoint the candle in an upward motion to call in protection.) Do not light yet.

Next, take your white sage and spiritually smoke your house to clear it of any residual energies that might hinder your protection work and to rid it of any negativity. Anoint the corner of the windowsills and door frames with a dab of the Wall of Fire Protection oil. You may replace white sage with other types of bundles if you prefer: rosemary, lavender, yerba santa, etc.

When the house is cleansed, light your candle while reciting the 27th psalm from the paper you carried with you while collecting your dirt. When the candle has finished burning, take the dirt and sprinkle around your property line as well as a little around your front and back doors.

PSALM 27
1 The Lord is my light and my salvation; I will fear no one. The Lord protects me from all danger; I will never be afraid. 2 When evil people attack me and try to kill me, they stumble and fall. 3 Even if a whole army surrounds me, I will not be afraid; even if enemies attack me, I will still trust God. 4 I have asked the Lord for one thing; one thing only do I want: to live in the Lord's house all my life, to marvel there at his goodness,

and to ask for his guidance. 5 In times of trouble he will shelter me; he will keep me safe in his Temple and make me secure on a high rock.6 So I will triumph over my enemies around me. With shouts of joy I will offer sacrifices in his Temple; I will sing, I will praise the Lord. 7Hear me, Lord, when I call to you! Be merciful and answer me! 8 When you said, "Come worship me," I answered, "I will come, Lord." 9Don't hide yourself from me! Don't be angry with me; don't turn your servant away. You have been my help; don't leave me, don't abandon me, O God, my savior. 10 My father and mother may abandon me, but the Lord will take care of me. 11 Teach me, Lord, what you want me to do, and lead me along a safe path, because I have many enemies. 12 Don't abandon me to my enemies, who attack me with lies and threats. 13 I know that I will live to see the Lord's goodness in this present life.14 Trust in the Lord. Have faith, do not despair. Trust in the Lord.

PORCH FLOORWASH

For protection of your home, mix your own urine with a bucket of water on a Monday, Wednesday, or Friday and wash your doorstep before dawn. When dry, sprinkle over with red brick dust. For extra protection, write the police captain's name on paper, burn it, and include the ashes in the wash.

RED BRICK DUST

Also called 'redding' or just plain ole 'brick dust,' it comes from an ancient belief in the spiritual powers of natural red ochre powder. It is often used as an ingredient in making floor washes to increase the power of protection and is usually scrubbed onto the front porch. Sprinkle a line down across doorways, and it is said that no one who means you harm can cross it.

CONCLUSION

I began writing this book three books ago, but something kept getting in my way, delaying it. I suppose I hesitated because, in the back of my mind, I wondered if publishing dark spells of destruction and sickness was the 'nice thing to do.' But, as a spell caster, I realize there can be no light without darkness. The only thing I ask is that you stop and pause before diving right into a hex or curse. Give it a cooling-off period of at least three days after the inciting incident before gathering your supplies – one week would be better. I want to add that I have never entertained the idea of casting a spell that would make someone ill or wish for their demise. For me, that is a sentence the Universe must decide. However, if someone has truly wronged you, I see no problem with seeking justice, sending them away, or making them excruciatingly uncomfortable for a bit of time. You decide.

BIBLIOGRAPHY

Illes, Judika. *Encyclopedia of 5,000 Spells – The Ultimate Reference Book for the Magical Arts.* Harper Collins. 2008.
Wright, Elbee. *Book of Legendary Spells.* Marlar Publishing Co. 1968.
Yronwode, Catherine & White, Gregory Lee. *Amulets, Charms, and Talismans in the Hoodoo and Conjure Tradition.* Lucky Mojo Curio Company Publishing. 2021.
Hyatt, Harry Middleton. *Hoodoo, Conjuration, Witchcraft, and Rootwork, Volumes 1 - 5.* Memoirs of the Alma C. Hyatt Foundation. 1970-1978.
Bacon, Alice. "Conjuring and Conjure-Doctors." *Southern Workman* Issue 28, 1895.
Oliver, Mark. "Unleashing the Power of the Gods: Hexes and Black Magic in the Ancient Greek Olympics." *Ancient Origins* July, 2017.
Giralt, Sebastia. "Medieval Necromancy – The Art of Controlling Demons." *Sciencia.cat.*
Downton, Dawn Rae. *The Little Book of Curses and Maledictions for Everyday Use.* Skyhorse Publishing. 2009.
White, Gregory Lee. *The Use of Magical Oils in Hoodoo, Prayer, and Spellwork.* White Willow Press. 2017.
White, Gregory Lee. *Casting Love Spells: Rituals of Love, Passion, and Attraction.* White Willow Press. 2022.
Johnson Smith & Co. *The Book of Forbidden Knowledge: Black Magic, Superstition, Charms, and Divination.* Circa 1920.
Gallagher, Ann-Marie. *The Spells Bible – The Definitive Guide to Charms and Enchantments.* Walking Stick Press. 2003.
Gordon, Stuart. *The Book of Curses: True Tales of Voodoo, Hoodoo, and Hex.* Brockhampton Press. 1994.
Jarus, Owen. "Black Magic Revealed in Two Ancient Curses." *LiveScience.* 2012.

Made in the USA
Monee, IL
01 August 2023